DK

TOP 10 ATHENS

Top 10 Athens Highlights

The Top 10 of Everything

CONTENTS

Athens Area by Area

Streetsmart

Within each Top 10 list in this book, no hierarchy of quality or popularity is implied. All 10 are, in the editor's opinion, of roughly equal merit.

The rate at which the world is changing is constantly keeping the DK travel team on our toes. While we've worked hard to ensure that this edition of Athens is accurate and up-to-date, we know that opening hours alter, standards shift, prices fluctuate, places close and new ones pop up in their stead. So, if you notice we've got something wrong or left something out, we want to hear about it. Please get in touch at **travelguides@dk.com**

BRETTOS

Welcome to Athens

Ancient temples and world-class museums. Sandy beaches and mouthwatering cuisine. Mediterranean sunshine and deep-blue skies. Athens brings together the best of ancient and contemporary Greece. It is dynamic, intriguing and exhilarating, and with DK Top 10 Athens, it's yours to explore.

We each have our own image of the magnificent **Parthenon** on the **Acropolis:** an ancient temple in a modern European capital. But it's not until you arrive in Athens that you realize how seamlessly the Ancient Greek monuments and ruins are integrated into Athens' contemporary urban life. Marble columns and carved pediments lie scattered in an Arcadian meadow next to a busy metro station – this is the **Ancient Agora**, at Thisio. The **National Archaeological Museum**, a proud Neo-Classical building, is filled with centuries-old treasures next to a street where walls are spray-painted with political slogans, on the edge of Exárhia. But Athens relishes these parallel worlds, and reveals new wonders at every turn.

The city sprawls in a wide valley, protected by rugged mountains, and opening to the south onto the glistening Aegean Sea. From the dense conglomeration of concrete apartment blocks rise two peaks: the aforementioned Acropolis and **Lykavittos Hill**, a rocky mound capped by a tiny church, which is enchantingly floodlit at night. And it is after dark that the city celebrates its passions for eating, drinking and enjoying life.

Whether you are visiting for a weekend or a week, our Top 10 guide brings together the best of everything the city has to offer from the historical **Philopappos Hill** to the stately **Temple of Olympian Zeus.** The guide has useful tips throughout, from seeking out what's free to avoiding the crowds, plus nine easy-to-follow itineraries, designed to tie together a clutch of sights in a short space of time. Add inspiring photography and detailed maps, and you've got the essential pocket-sized travel companion. **Enjoy the book, and enjoy Athens.**

Clockwise from top: **Odeon of Herodes Atticus; Osios Loukas mosaic, Delphi; Brettos, Plaka; Acropolis; Fresco in Kesariani Monastery; Olympic Stadium; National Archaeological Museum**

Exploring Athens

Athens offers a vast range of things to do and see, both ancient and modern. Here are some ideas of how to make the most of your time. The city centre is relatively compact, so you should be able to do most of your sightseeing on foot if you don't want to use public transport.

Colourful Plaka is the place to shop for traditional souvenirs.

Two Days in Athens

Day ❶

MORNING

Begin with Athens' centrepiece, the **Acropolis** *(see pp12–13)*, crowned by the Parthenon. See finds from the site at the **Acropolis Museum** *(see pp14–15)*, then lunch at the museum café.

AFTERNOON

Follow the **Dionysiou Areopagitou walkway** *(see p60)* around the Acropolis to the **Ancient Agora** *(see pp16–19)*. Walk to **Platia Monastirakiou** *(see p86)*, stopping in at **Benaki Museum of Islamic Art** *(see p88)* for great textiles and ceramics, then hunt for souvenirs in **Plaka** *(see p79)*.

EVENING

Dine on modern Greek fare in the hip **Psyrri** *(see p90)* neighbourhood.

Day ❷

MORNING

Explore the **Varvakios Central Market** *(see p94)* and visit the **Hyper-Hypo** bookstore *(see p89)* nearby. Then walk to Ermou, stopping at the **Kapnikarea Church** *(see p87)* on the way. Continue to Syntagma, home to the **Parliament** *(see p101)*. Walk through the **National Gardens** *(see p101)* to the **Benaki Museum of Greek Culture** *(see pp26–7)*. Lunch in Kolonaki.

AFTERNOON

Walk, or take the cable car, up **Lykavittos Hill** *(see p102)* for fabulous

city views, then cross Exarheia to arrive at the **National Archaeological Museum** *(see pp20–21)*.

EVENING

After an aperitif at the **TAF** bar-gallery *(see p82)*, have dinner in Plaka, below the floodlit Acropolis.

Four Days in Athens

Day 1

MORNING

Begin with the **Acropolis** *(see pp12–13)*, then see magnificent findings at the **Acropolis Museum** *(see pp14–15)*.

AFTERNOON

Proceed to the **Ancient Agora** *(see pp16–19)* for more ancient history, then explore the cafés and souvenir shops in pretty **Plaka** *(see p79)*, also checking out the **Roman Forum and Tower of the Winds** *(see pp24–5)*.

The Parthenon sits atop the Acropolis hill, overlooking Athens.

Day 2

MORNING

See the **Kerameikos** *(see pp30–31)* archaeological site, then wander through the busy **Varvakios Central Market** *(see p94)*. Walk up Ermou, stopping at the church of **Kapnikarea** *(see p87)*, then proceed to Kolonaki.

AFTERNOON

Visit the **Byzantine and Christian Museum** *(see pp32–3)* and the nearby **Museum of Cycladic Art** *(see pp22–3)*, pausing at either of their lovely cafés. Afterwards, head to Dexameni *(see p107)* for an ouzo or meze.

Day 3

MORNING

Visit the **National Archaeological Museum** *(see pp20–21)*.

AFTERNOON

Catch the tram to **Glyfada** *(see p129)* and relax on the beach. If it's too cold to swim, head for the thermal waters of **Lake Vouliagmeni** *(see p129)*.

Day 4

MORNING

Visit the **Museum of Greek Musical Instruments** *(see p78)* in Plaka. Explore **Philopappos Hill** *(see pp34–5)* and the **Temple of Olympian Zeus** *(see pp36–7)*, then walk through the **National Gardens** *(see p101)* to Kolonaki.

AFTERNOON

Visit the **Benaki Museum of Greek Culture** *(see pp26–7)*. Hike up **Lykavittos Hill** *(see p102)* for views over the city.

Top 10 Athens Highlights

The Parthenon, on the Acropolis

TOP 10 Athens Highlights

Athens is both the Classical, marble-pillared cradle of Western civilization and a modern urban sprawl of concrete and traffic. Between these extremes lies a vibrant city, where the influences of East and West entwine in the markets, cafés and tavernas, which are built upon ancient ruins and rub shoulders with multi-domed Byzantine churches.

1 Acropolis

The crown jewel of Greece, if not all of Europe. Its temples are among the most influential buildings in Western architecture *(see pp12–15)*.

2 The Ancient Agora

The likes of Socrates, Aristotle and St Paul all held forth in the marketplace below the Acropolis. This was the heart of the ancient city *(see pp16–19)*.

3 National Archaeological Museum

Finds from some of the world's greatest cultures are housed here. Exhibits include the gold treasure of Mycenae and the first sculptures to depict the complexity of the human form *(see pp20–21)*.

4 Museum of Cycladic Art

This museum houses one of the largest collections of Cycladic art in the world, showcasing early Bronze Age marble statuettes, vases and tools, which still inspire artists today *(see pp22–3)*.

5 Roman Forum and Tower of the Winds

The Romans abandoned the Ancient Agora and created this orderly new commercial centre. Its showpiece was the magnificent Tower of the Winds *(see pp24–5)*.

Benaki Museum of Greek Culture 6

This first-rate collection of Greek art from Neolithic times to the present is housed in a beautifully restored Neo-Classical mansion. It has several annexes, including the nearby Ghika Gallery *(see pp26–7)*.

7 Kerameikos

Classical Athens' cemetery gives a fascinating cross-section of life, and death, at the city's edge, with elaborate tombs, temples, sacred roads – and an ancient brothel *(see pp30–31)*.

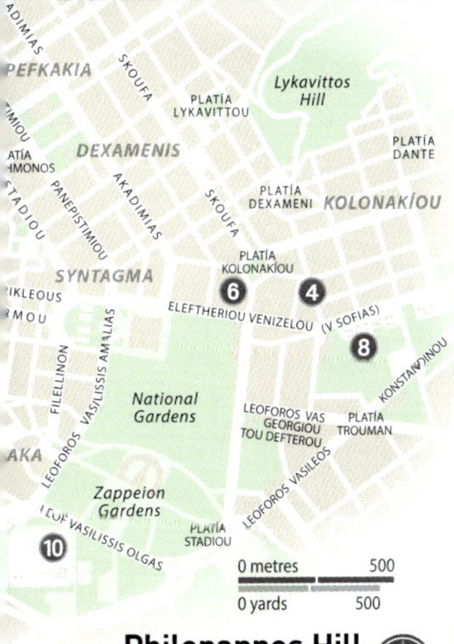

8 Byzantine and Christian Museum

The Byzantine and Christian heritage of the entire Greek world is told through examples of its works, from the intricacy of precious metalwork to the solemnity of the many icons *(see pp32–3)*.

Philopappos Hill 9

A green-gladed respite in the city centre, with a wonderful view and a mix of monuments ranging from ancient and Byzantine to modern *(see pp34–5)*.

10 Temple of Olympian Zeus

Ancient Greece's most colossal temple stands beside the monumental arch with inscriptions honouring Greek hero Theseus on one side and Roman emperor Hadrian *(see pp36–7)* on the other.

Acropolis

One of the most famous archaeological sites in the world, the Acropolis and its breathtaking monuments stand as a testament to the political and cultural achievements of Greece. The great marble masterpieces here were constructed during the late 5th-century BCE reign of Perikles, the Golden Age of Athens. Most were temples built to honour Athena, the city's patron goddess. Still awe-inspiring for their proportion and scale, the temples were adorned with magnificent sculptures of gods, many of which survive today.

1 Acropolis Rock

The highest point in Athens, this 160-m- (525-ft-) high limestone outcrop **(main image)** forms the foundation of the Acropolis, earning the site the moniker "Sacred Rock".

6 Erechtheion

Poseidon and Athena are said to have battled for patronage of Athens on this spot. The Erechtheion's design combines temples to each of the two gods **(above)**.

2 Temple of Athena Nike ("Victory")

There has been a temple **(above)** to a goddess of victory at this location since prehistoric times, as it protects and stands over the most vulnerable part of the rock.

3 Propylaia

At the top of the rock, you are greeted by the Propylaia, the grand entrance through which all visitors passed to reach the summit temples.

4 Panathenaic Way

The route used in an ancient procession during which a new tunic, or *peplos*, would have been offered to Athena, along with sacrifices.

5 Parthenon

The epitome of ancient Greek Classical art, a magnificent "Temple to the Virgin", goddess Athena **(left)**. She was represented inside by a giant gold and ivory sculpture.

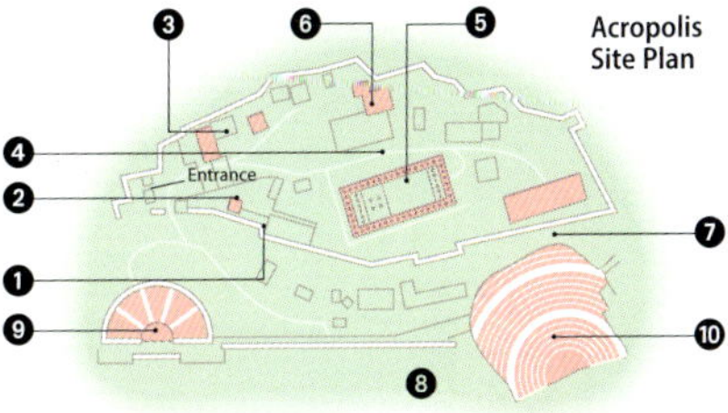

7 Choragic Monument of Thrasyllos

Originally dedicated to the god of wine, this cave with pillars became the church of the Mother of God of the Golden Cave (Panagia Chrysospiliotissa).

8 Acropolis Museum

The Acropolis Museum *(see pp14–15)* houses around 4,000 artifacts in a vast space that reflects the splendour of the ancient monument.

9 Odeon of Herodes Atticus

Built in 161 CE by its namesake, this open-air theatre hosts events of the Epidauros Athens Festival *(see pp72–3)*.

THE ACROPOLIS IN LATER TIMES

In the 5th century CE, the Parthenon was used as a church. During the Ottoman occupation, it was used as a mosque, and the Erechtheion as a harem. The Ottomans also kept gunpowder in the Parthenon, which led to its near destruction when the Venetians shelled it in 1687 *(see p35)*. The Parthenon suffered further damage from 1800 to 1803 when Lord Elgin removed sculptures, architectural features and inscriptions, to take them to England.

10 Dionysos Theatre

Associated with the cult of Dionysus Eleutherius, this vast theatre **(below)** could hold over 17,000 people. Here, works of dramatists such as Aristophanes Menander, Sophocles, Aeschylus and Euripides enthralled ancient Athenians, creating an enduring cultural legacy.

NEED TO KNOW

MAP J5 ■ www.odysseus.culture.gr

Open summer: 8am–8pm daily (winter: to 5pm; shoulder season: hours vary, check website); last entry: 30 mins before closing

Adm €30; reduced €15 (Nov–Mar: all adm: €10)

Acropolis Museum: **MAP K5**; Dionysiou Areopagitou 15; open Apr–Oct: 9am–8pm daily (to 5pm Mon, to 10pm Fri); Nov–Mar: hours vary, check website; adm €20; www.theacropolismuseum.gr

■ A timed ticketing system *(www.hhticket.gr)* regulates the number of visitors, protects the monument and ensures a better experience.

■ The Acropolis is accessible via an elevator for those with limited mobility. There are also some paved paths at the site.

Acropolis Museum

The Caryatids

1 The Caryatids

The original statued pillars that supported the Erechtheion's porch have been brought inside. Their arms are broken now, but initially they held libation bowls.

2 The Parthenon Marbles

The marbles are displayed in the order in which they would have graced the Parthenon, with blank spaces significantly left for sculptures that remain in London.

3 The Calf-Bearer

This joyous Archaic sculpture shows a bearded man carrying a calf, to be offered as a sacrifice to Athena. The statue itself was a votive offering and dates to 570 BCE.

4 The Peplos Kore

One of the most exquisite of the Archaic votive statues. Her gown, called a *peplos*, was painted with decorative colours. Traces of paint are still visible on her eyes, lips and curly hair.

5 Kore with Almond-Shaped Eyes

The most sumptuous of the votive *korai* – her detailed drapery and fully formed body show real development in sculpture. Her dress was painted with detailed patterns, including a border with the distinctive "Greek key" pattern.

6 Pediment of the Ancient Temple

Part of the pediment of an ancient temple to Athena, built before the Parthenon and later destroyed, shows Athena fighting against a Titan. It dates to 520 BCE.

7 The Kritios Boy

This sculpture of a young male athlete marks the transition from Archaic to early Classical sculpture, with the introduction of a naturalistic pose. The Kritios Boy sculpture dates to 480 BCE.

The "Mourning Athena"

8 Relief of the "Mourning Athena"

This tiny relief shows the goddess Athena as a girl, without sword or shield and clad in an Attic *peplos*.

9 The Glass Floor

The museum has been built directly over an early Christian settlement. Glass floors allow visitors to look directly down into the site while approaching the museum entrance from the street.

10 Frieze on the Temple of Athena Nike

The small but dynamically sculpted frieze shows scenes of battle, with gods, Persians and Greeks all stepping into the fray.

MORE THAN A BUILDING

Parthenon marble

In mid-2008, the Acropolis Museum opened with much anticipation. Finally, the treasures of the Acropolis had a befittingly beautiful space to house them. However, there was a greater motive to the construction of this museum – to send a pointed international message. Between 1800 and 1803, the seventh Earl of Elgin removed two-thirds of the sculptures (or marbles) of gods, men and monsters adorning the Parthenon and took them to England. Most of these pieces are now in the British Museum, which refuses to return them. The Acropolis Museum has answered previous criticism that Athens could not display them adequately or safely, for a special room awaits the return. Public pressure to return the marbles has mounted in recent years, and in March 2023, the Vatican returned parts of the marbles to Greece. Negotiations with the British Museum commenced in 2021, but were undercut by former UK Prime Minister Rishi Sunak who prevented the marbles' return. Greece continues to hope that the rise in visitors to the Acropolis Museum will increase pressure on Britain. A 2024 poll showed that 53 per cent of British citizens were in favour of returning the Parthenon Marbles.

TOP 10 SCENES DEPICTED IN THE PARTHENON MARBLES

1 The birth of Athena, springing fully formed out of Zeus's head *(see p52)*

2 The Pantheon watching Athena's birth

3 Athena and Poseidon's fight for control of the city *(see p52)*

4 The gods watch and take sides in Athena and Poseidon's battle

5 The Panathenaic Procession, ancient Athens' most important religious event

6 The battle of the Centaurs and Lapiths

7 The battle of the gods and the Titans

8 The battle of the Greeks and the Amazons

9 The sack of Troy

10 Priestesses prepare a veil for Athena

At the Acropolis Museum, the Parthenon Marbles are displayed with pride of place in a special glass-walled chamber. Empty spaces or replicas stand in for the marbles still retained at the British Museum and elsewhere.

The Ancient Agora

Founded in the 6th century BCE, Athens' ancient marketplace was the heart of the city for 1,200 years. It was the centre for all civic activities, including politics, commerce, philosophy, religion, arts and athletics. This is where Socrates addressed his public, where democracy was born and where St Paul preached. Because of its varied uses, the rambling site can be confusing. However, compared to the sweltering Acropolis, the grassy Ancient Agora is a relaxing place to wander, as you imagine the lively bustle that once filled it.

1 Temple of Hephaistos

Greece's best-preserved Classical temple **(above)** is devoted to Hephaistos, god of fire and metal work, and Athena Ergani, protectress of potters and cottage industries.

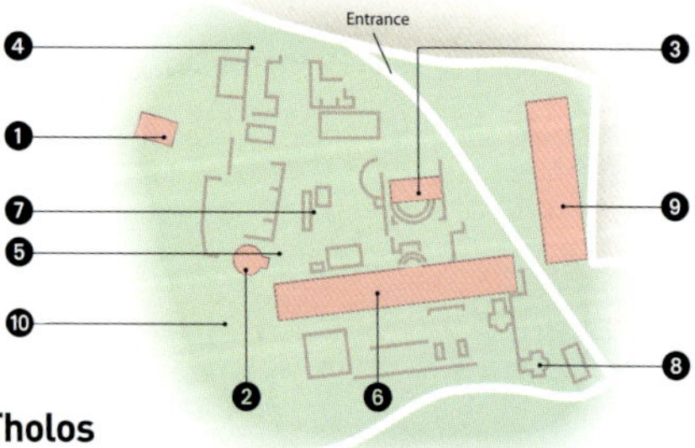

Ancient Agora Site Plan

2 Tholos

The executive committee of the first parliament lived and worked in this circular building, also known as the Prytaneion.

3 Odeon of Agrippa

Marcus Vipsanius Agrippa, an official with the first emperor Augustus, had this theatre built in 15 CE. Outside stood statues of three serpent-tailed Giants and Tritons on huge plinths **(left)**. Two Tritons and a Giant remain.

4 Stoa Basileios

Built in 500 BCE, this building housed the office of legal affairs concerning ancient cults. Most of it was destroyed when the Heruli invaded and sacked Athens in 267 CE. Its ruins are best viewed from Adrianou.

5 Monument of the Eponymous Heroes

Citizens were divided into 10 tribes *(phylae)*, each represented by a different Attican hero. Dated 350 BCE, this monument had bronze statues of each representative tribal hero: Antiochos, Ajax, Kekrops, Hippothoon, Erechtheus, Aigeas, Leos, Akamas, Pandion and Oeneus.

NEED TO KNOW

MAP B4 ■ Adrianou 24, Monastiraki ■ www.odysseusculture.gr

Open summer: 8am–7:30pm daily (winter: to 5pm; shoulder season: hours vary); last entry: 30 mins before closing

Adm €20 summer, €10 reduced & winter

■ The best overview of the Ancient Agora is from the Areopagos rock *(see p61)*.

■ Head to the local favourite Dioskouri, situated at Dioskouron 13, to enjoy a coffee or light meal and a great view of the Ancient Agora.

6 Middle Stoa

The large Middle Stoa **(above)** took up the major part of the central marketplace, its aisles lined with Doric columns.

7 Altar of Zeus Agoraios

This lavish temple to the ruler of the gods was originally built elsewhere in Athens (possibly the Pnyx) in the 4th century BCE. In the first century CE, it was dismantled, brought to the Ancient Agora and reconstructed.

8 Nymphaion

The ruins of the Nymphaion, an elaborate 2nd-century fountain-house, are still visible, despite the building of Agii Apostoli church over it in the 11th century.

SITE OF PILGRIMAGE

You may well see people on the Areopagos, the rock above the Ancient Agora, praying or singing hymns. This is the site named in the Bible (Acts 17:22–34) where St Paul gave his "Sermon to an Unknown God" that spoke of the errors of ancient Greek religions. He also converted the first Athenians to Christianity, including Dionysios the Areopagite, here. The site remains a port of call for pilgrims retracing St Paul's steps.

10 Great Drain

When it rains heavily, the Great Drain **(above)** still collects runoff from the Acropolis and Ancient Agora, and sends it to the now usually dry Eridanos river.

9 Stoa of Attalos

King Attalos II of Pergamon (159–138 BCE) built this impressive two-storey structure **(above)**. It was reconstructed in 1956 by the American School of Archaeology. Today the Stoa is a fine museum displaying finds from the Ancient Agora *(see pp18–19)*.

Agora Museum (Stoa of Attalos)

1 Head of Nike

This small, delicate head of Athena Nike, dated to about 425 BCE, was once covered with sheets of silver and gold; eyes would have been inset.

2 Klepsydra

Dating back to the 5th century BCE, this is a unique example of the terracotta water clocks used for timing speeches in the public law courts. When a speaker began, the stopper was pulled out of the jug. It would take exactly six minutes for the water to run out, at which point the speaker had to stop, even if he was in mid-sentence.

Aryballos

3 Ostraka

These small inscribed pottery fragments played a crucial role in the incipient democracy. Called *ostraka*, they were used as ballots in the process of ostracism. When there was fear of a tyranny, citizens voted to exile politicians considered dangerous to democracy. Those displayed show the names of several prominent politicians exiled in this way, including Themistokles, one of Athens' most important leaders.

Ostraka fragments

4 Bronze Shield

This huge Spartan shield was a trophy taken by the Athenians after their victory over the Spartans in the battle of Sphacteria, in 425 BCE. It is a vast object, and it is difficult to imagine a soldier carrying something so heavy and cumbersome into the melee of battle. On the front of the shield, one of the Athenian victors has inscribed, "Athens defeated Sparta at Pylos".

5 Aryballos

This small Archaic oil-flask sculpted in the form of a kneeling boy represents an athlete binding a ribbon, a symbol of victory, around his head. It dates to around 530 BCE.

6 Winged Nike

This sensuous, swirling, rippling statue of Athena once adorned the Agora's Stoa of Zeus Eleutherios. Her active stance and clinging, flowing *chiton* (a loose, full-length tunic) are typical of the way in which the goddess was depicted at that time. It dates to around 415 BCE.

7 Apollo Patroös

This colossal, finely sculpted marble cult statue of Apollo graced a temple to the god in the Ancient Agora. Dating to around 335 BCE, it is the work of the Greek sculptor and painter Euphranor. Although the statue is damaged, its design suggests that the god of music was depicted playing the kithara, an early stringed instrument.

Apollo Patroös

8 Athenian Law for Democracy

In 337 or 336 BCE, the *Ekklesia* (an assembly of the citizens of Athens) passed the historic anti-tyranny decree, giving each male citizen the right to vote. The inscription is accompanied by a marble relief celebrating the *demos* – the people of Athens.

9 Marble Kleroterion

This device was used by the Parliament of Athens between the 3rd and 2nd century BCE, in the period of the ten tribes of Attica, to select people randomly for official roles. The seemingly simple box performed operations with slots, weights, cranks and coloured balls. A sign below the display case explains the complexities of its operation.

10 Calyx Krater

Dating to 530 BCE, this is the earliest known calyx krater – an elegant vessel used to mix water and wine at banquets – and the only vase of this shape attributed to Exekias, the greatest Attic vase painter. It shows several beautifully detailed scenes, including Herakles being introduced to the gods of Olympos and the Greek and Trojan heroes' fight over the body of Patroklos.

THE STOA OF ATTALOS

The Stoa of Attalos was originally a 2nd-century BCE shopping mall. Both arcades were divided into shops, and the cool marble-pillared space was a popular place for wealthy Athenians to meet and gossip. Through decades of excavations, the Ancient Agora has become recognized as one of Greece's most important sites, yielding finds precious for their artistic quality and ability to tell important stories about political and cultural life in the first democracy. During the 1950s, the American School of Archaeology reconstructed the Stoa and converted the building into a museum to display finds from the site. Most of the museum's exhibits are closely connected with the development of democracy in Athens. Outside, in the marble passage, statues that once adorned the temples in the marketplace are displayed.

Head of Nike

The reconstructed Stoa of Attalos, home of the Agora Museum

TOP 10 National Archaeological Museum

More than just the best museum in Greece, this is one of the most important and exciting museums in the world. It is packed with famous, influential and beautiful works, from the Neolithic Age, to the great Bronze Age cultures described by Homer, to the halcyon days of Classical Athens, up to the Roman era. Highlights include numerous gold artefacts found at Mycenae and elegant Archaic *kouroi* and *korai* statues.

1 Cycladic Collection, 3200–2200 BCE

The Cycladic Museum *(see pp22–3)* has the largest collection from this civilization, but here you'll find some of the most unusual pieces, such as this harp-player **(above)**, showing, unusually, a three-dimensional figure in action.

2 Thera Frescoes

The highly advanced settlement of Akrotiri, on the ancient island of Thera (now Santorini), was buried after a major volcanic eruption in the 17th century BCE. Beautiful frescoes, such as these boxer boys **(right)**, were perfectly preserved under the ash.

3 Archaic Kouroi/Korai, 7th Century BCE–480 BCE

Used in temples and graves, these statues of idealised youths and maidens were the first monumental works in Greek art. The earliest are stiff and stylized, but through the 6th century, artists learnt to depict the body more naturally.

4 Mycenaean Collection, 16th–11th Centuries BCE

The Mycenaeans were famed for their prowess as warriors and for the gold amassed by their traders. Parts of those hoards are displayed here, including the "Mask of Agamemnon" **(right)** and priceless swords and jewellery.

5 Bronze Collection

This, the richest collection of bronze works from the Archaic and Classical eras, includes a majestic 460 BCE sculpture of Poseidon or Zeus **(left)**, a 140 BCE sculpture of a galloping horse and a youth of Antikythira.

6 Classical Statuary

The collection features sculptures from temples all around Greece. Highlights include those from the Temple of Asklepios at Epidauros, and a relief depicting the Eleusinian Mysteries (a myth centred around the abduction of Persephone, daughter of Demeter, the goddess of harvest, by Hades, god of the Underworld).

7 Hellenistic Statuary

Here the stiff monuments of the Archaic period give way to sculptures that are full of vigorous movement and sensuality. This is especially so in the 100 BCE group of Aphrodite, Pan and Eros, and the statue of a wounded Gaul.

8 Vases and Minor Art Collection

The collection contains impressive vases, terracotta figurines, gold jewels and glass vessels, dated from the 10th century BCE up to the 18th century CE.

9 Egyptian Wing

This collection, from the Neolithic period to the end of the Roman era, is fascinating to view in conjunction with the earliest Greek Archaic art, which borrowed from Egyptian statuary before developing its very own style. The collection includes a funerary boat sculpted from wood **(below)**.

PRESERVATION DURING WORLD WAR II

During World War II, a team led by Greek architect Anastasios Orlandos protected the museum's artifacts by temporarily hiding them in concrete trenches and underground bunkers. When German forces entered the museum, they only found empty halls.

10 Grave Stelae

Classical marble grave sculptures **(below)** became so opulent by the end of the 4th century BCE that they were banned. The scenes in these beautiful carvings typically show the deceased on the right, the bereaved on the left.

NEED TO KNOW

MAP C1 ■ 44 Patision (28 Oktovriou) ■ www.namuseum.gr

Open Apr–Oct: 1–8pm Tue, 8am–8pm Wed–Mon; Nov–Mar: 1–8pm Tue, 8:30am–3:30pm Wed–Mon

Adm €12

■ There's so much to explore at the National Archaeological Museum that it makes sense to visit it twice. The museum's informational guide book is a great purchase.

■ There's an atrium café inside, and a larger one in the plaza out front.

Museum of Cycladic Art

This modern museum has one of the world's finest collections of Cycladic art. It brings together a fantastic selection of ancient Greek art spanning 5,000 years of history. Dating back to the 3rd millennium BCE, the Cycladic marble sculptures depicting women and men have a haunting simplicity that inspired many 20th-century artists and sculptors, including Picasso, Henry Moore and Modigliani.

1 Dove Vase

Carved entirely from one block of marble, this vase, decorated with doves **(above)**, is the most remarkable of a series of vessels found in tombs. Archaeologists believe birds held an important meaning for the Cycladic culture, since they appear in many other carvings as well – but the nature of that significance remains to be established.

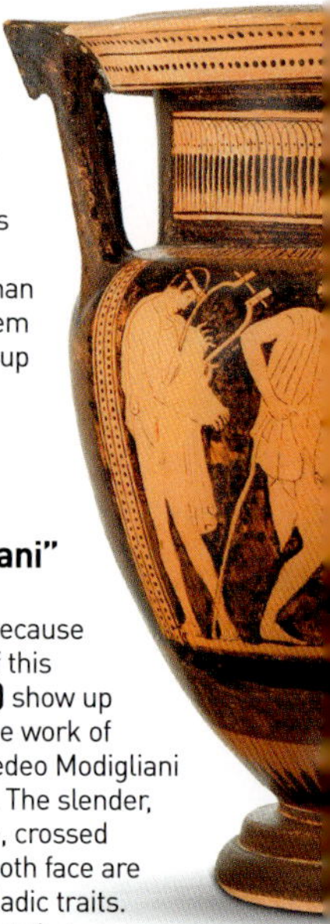

2 Red-Figure Column Krater

This vase **(right)**, attributed to the Agrigento Painter, active in Attica in the 5th century BCE, shows a girl musician playing a double flute and a young man holding a lyre. Between them is a dancing youth. The group is led by an ivy-wreathed boy carrying an amphora on his shoulders.

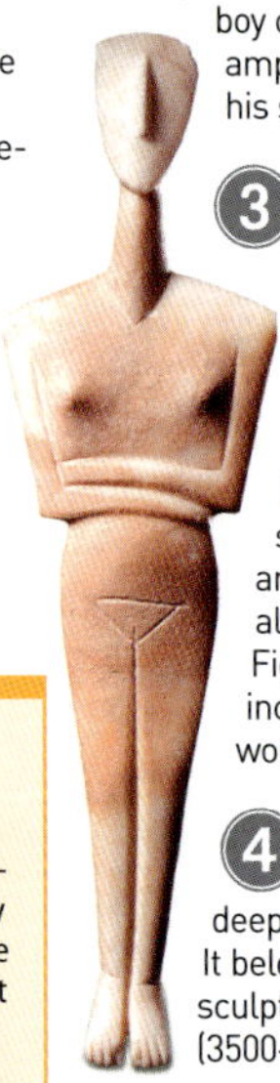

3 "Modigliani" Figure

So-called because the lines of this figure **(left)** show up clearly in the work of painter Amedeo Modigliani (1884–1920). The slender, simple shape, crossed arms and smooth face are all classic Cycladic traits. Figures with feet that are incapable of support indicate that they would probably have been lying down.

4 Female Figurine

The limestone female figurine has deep eye sockets and modelled breasts. It belongs to a group of human-form sculptures from the Chalcolithic period (3500–2800 BCE in the Cyclades).

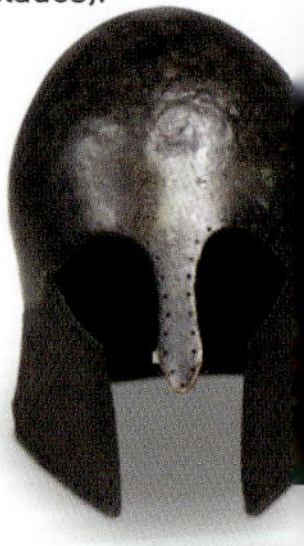

5 Bronze Helmets

The Corinthian helmet **(right)** underwent quite a development in the 7th century BCE, with the shape being progressively altered in order to fit better on the head. It was the first helmet to be fashioned from a single bronze sheet, and it protected every part of the head.

THE GOULANDRIS DYNASTY

The Goulandris family are prominent benefactors. Nikolaos and Dolly Goulandris founded the Museum of Cycladic Art in 1986. The Museum of Natural History, in the Kifissia district, was founded by Angelos and Niki Goulandris in 1965. Most recently, the Basil and Elise Goulandris Foundation has opened two contemporary museums – on Andros in 1979, and in 2019 in Athens *(see p49)*.

6 Symposium Kylix

This exceptional piece of 5th-century BCE pottery **(below)** shows a naked youth drawing wine from a large mixing vessel, known as a krater, to fill the cup he holds in his left hand. According to the inscription, the young man is named Lysis, and his beauty is praised by the addition of the epithet "fair".

Museum of Cycladic Art Floorplan

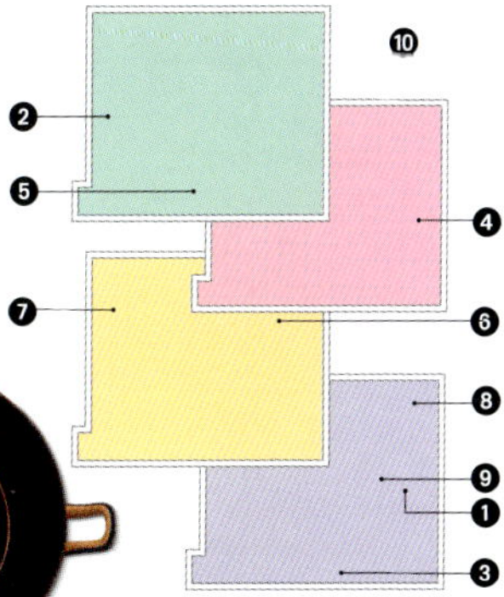

Key to Floorplan

- Cycladic Art
- Ancient Greek Art
- Ancient Cypriot Art
- Scenes from Daily Life in Antiquity

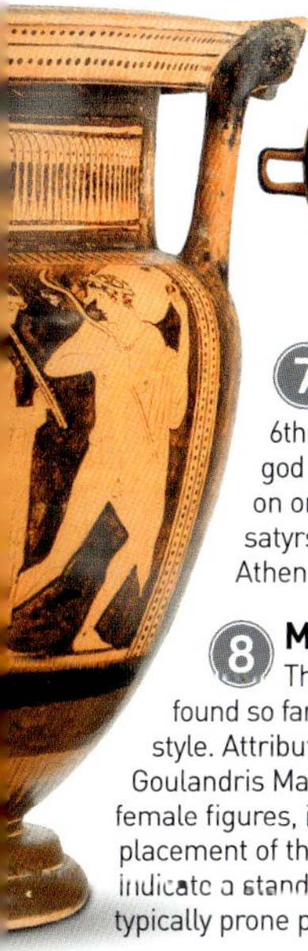

7 Dionysos Vase

This beautifully preserved 6th-century BCE vase shows the god of wine and revelry Dionysos on one side (flanked by dancing satyrs) and, on the other side, Athena and Hermes conversing.

8 Male Figure

The only male figure of its size found so far in the prototypical Cycladic style. Attributed by some scholars to the Goulandris Master, who created the finest female figures, it has the same shape and placement of the arms. The separated legs indicate a standing pose, rather than the typically prone pose of the female figures.

9 Hunter-Warrior and Queen

This male figure, with his elongated arms and almond-shaped eyes, is among the most naturalistic of the later Cycladic figures. Experts believe that the dagger carved around the figure indicates that he was a hunter-warrior.

NEED TO KNOW

MAP P3 ■ Neofytou Douka 4 and Vasilissis Sofias ■ www.cycladic.gr

Open 10am–5pm Wed–Mon (to 8pm Thu, from 11am Sun)

Adm €12 (€9 reduced); adm for special exhibitions varies

■ **All the featured exhibits are found in the main building of the Cycladic Wing, while the Stathatos Mansion shows temporary exhibitions.**

■ **It's best to visit until after 1pm as mornings are crowded with tour groups.**

■ **The museum's atrium café serves delicious Cycladic-inspired dishes for a light lunch.**

10 Stathatos Mansion

In 1991, the museum took over the adjoining Stathatos Mansion **(above)**, a gilded Neo-Classical confection by Bavarian architect Ernst Ziller *(see p102)*. Here the museum hosts all temporary exhibitions, receptions and lectures.

Roman Forum and Tower of the Winds

During the first century CE, the Romans moved Athens' marketplace here from the old Agora. Smaller than the original, the marble-pillared courtyard was a grander place to set up shop, and this became the city's commercial and administrative centre until the 19th century. Its greatest attraction was the unique and brilliantly designed Tower of the Winds.

1 Byzantine Grave Markers

In Byzantine times, when the Tower of the Winds was used as a church, the area around it was a cemetery. Graves were marked with cylindrical engraved markers, some of which were quite beautiful. These were later gathered in one place, along with others from around Athens.

2 Vespasianae (68-seat Public Latrine)

The pleasantly situated marble facility was housed in a rectangular building with a courtyard in the middle, and latrines lining all four sides. Proximity wasn't a problem – latrines were social gathering places.

3 Tower of the Winds

The octagonal tower **(left)**, built by Syrian astronomer Andronikos Kyrrhestas in 50 BCE, has personifications of the eight winds on each side. Inside, a water clock was operated by a stream from the Acropolis.

4 Fethiye Mosque

During the Ottoman occupation, the Forum remained important. This "Mosque of the Conquest" was built soon after Sultan Mehmet II took Athens in June 1456. After its long restoration, the interior has been opened for visitors.

5 Courtyard

This was the centre of activity. The courtyard was surrounded by shops and workshops selling food, cloth, ceramics, jewellery and wares from abroad. The Emperor Hadrian had the courtyard paved in the 2nd century CE.

6 Fountain

This splashing marble fountain **(below)**, whose waters, like those of the water clock, may also have been sourced from the Acropolis, once provided cool relief to market-goers. But stay away from the brackish water that occasionally fills it today.

7 Gate of Athena Archegetis

The four-columned western entrance to the forum **(left)** is built of Pentelic marble. It was dedicated by the people of Athens to the goddess Athena in her avatar of Archegetis, "(S)he Who Commands".

A MISCELLANY OF FINDS

Ever since the 1940s, archaeologists have used the forum as a repository for small, unclassifiable finds from all over Attica. Thus the site is studded with out-of-place but fascinating extras, such as the wall of mismatched capital pieces near the Vespasianae, and the garlanded sarcophagus, about which little is known, by the fountain.

Roman columns and the Fethiye Mosque behind

8 East Propylon

This is one of the two original entrances to the marketplace. In a stoa next to it are sculptures of important Romans, probably officials or emperors, which market-goers would have seen while coming and going.

9 Agoranomeion

This two-roomed building was long believed to be the office of market officials. Latest theories reckon it was a part of a cult to Athena Archegetis or all Roman emperors.

NEED TO KNOW

MAP J4–K4 ■ Monastiraki
■ www.odysseus.culture.gr

Open summer: 8am–8pm daily (winter: to 3pm; shoulder season: hours vary, check website); last entry: 30 minutes before closing

Adm €10 summer, €5 reduced & winter

■ **During the August full moon, the Roman Forum and many other sites stay open till late and are free of charge. They may also host free cultural events.**

■ **Head to O Platanos** ***(see p83)*****, a five-minute walk from the Forum, for a classic taverna experience in a square shaded by trees.**

Roman Forum Map

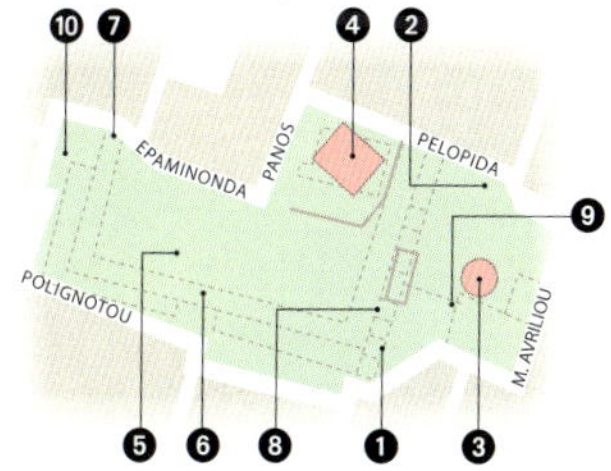

10 Inscription on Gate of Athena Archegetis

A faint inscription on the *architrave* (the horizontal architectural structure at the top) commemmorates the contruction of this gate between 11 to 9 BCE by the citizens of Athens, during the term of the archon Nikias.

Benaki Museum of Greek Culture

This comprehensive museum covers Greek history from the Stone Age (7000 BCE) to the 20th century, by way of Classical Greece and the Byzantine and Ottoman empires. Here, over 20,000 objects show the evolution of Greek painting, sculpture and handicrafts.

1 Paintings by El Greco

Domenikos Theotokopoulos (1541–1614) became known as El Greco in Spain. Two early works here, completed while the artist was still in his homeland of Crete, include *St Luke Painting the Panagia Odigitria* **(left)**, painted between 1560 and 1567.

2 Thebes Treasure

During the late Bronze Age, ornamental jewellery was used to display personal wealth. This hoard of Mycenaean gold jewellery includes an engraved gold signet ring, depicting a sacred marriage connected to the worship of a prehistoric goddess.

3 Thessaly Treasure

This stunning display of Hellenistic gold jewellery from the 3rd–2nd centuries BCE employs filigree and granulation (beads of gold soldered onto metal) to produce minutely crafted earrings, necklaces, bracelets and diadems. One of the highlights is a decorative band with a knot of Herakles at its centre.

4 The Building

This Neo-Classical mansion of 1867 **(above)** was bought by Emmanuel Benakis in 1910, passed to his children, and then presented to the state in 1931 when it opened as a museum.

5 Mid-18th-Century Reception Room

The richly painted ceiling and panelled walls of this room **(below)** – a reconstruction from a Macedonian mansion in Kozani – recall a time when these crafts flourished locally.

6 Café

Cultural overload? Take a break on the rooftop terrace café overlooking the trees and lawns of the National Gardens.

NEED TO KNOW

MAP N3
■ Koumbari 1, Kolonaki
■ www.benaki.gr

Open 10am–6pm Wed–Mon (to midnight Thu, to 4pm Sun)

Adm €12 permanent exhibits; €9 temporary exhibits (€6 reduced); under 22s free

■ The admission to the permanent collection is free Thursdays from 6pm to midight.

■ The Benaki Museum has a lovely café on the terrace with views of the National Gardens – an ideal place to break for lunch in the middle of taking in the excellent collection.

7 Évia Treasure

Around 3000 BCE, the introduction of metallurgy marked the transition from the Stone Age to the Bronze Age. Outstanding examples from this period are three cups, two gold **(below)** and one silver, hammered into simple forms with minimal decoration. They date from between 3000 and 2800 BCE.

8 A Second Room

Another reconstruction from Macedonia, this mid-19th-century reception room from Kozani features a minutely carved wooden ceiling, ornate built-in wooden cupboards and a low seating area, complete with delicate Persian rugs and cushions, and a wrought-iron coffee table.

WHO WAS BENAKIS?

Antonis Benakis (1873–1954) was born in Egypt to an immensely wealthy merchant, Emmanuel Benakis, who later served as Mayor of Athens from 1914 to 1916. Antonis began collecting Islamic art while in Alexandria and went on to collect Byzantine art and Greek folk art once his family moved to Athens. He donated the entire collection to the Greek state in 1931. His sister, Penelope Delta (1874–1941), was a much-loved author of children's books.

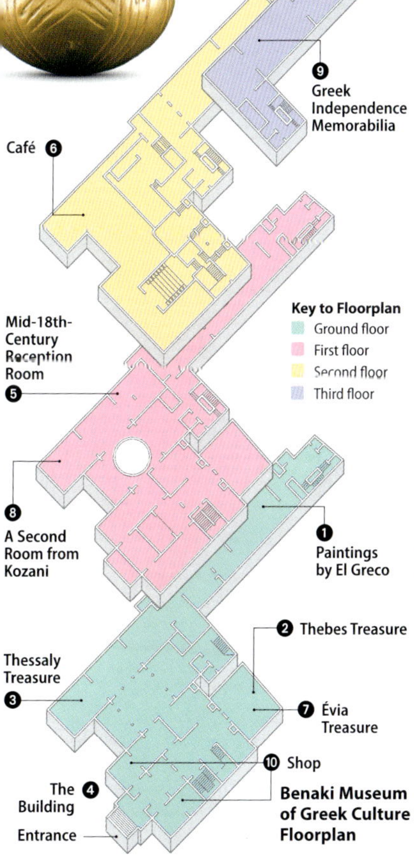

Benaki Museum of Greek Culture Floorplan

9 Greek Independence Memorabilia

Finely decorated swords, sabres and rifles, a painting of a freedom fighter from 1821, the flag of Hydra island **(below)** proclaiming "either victory or death", and a writing desk belonging to Lord Bryon are among the displays.

10 Shop

Here, exhibits such as ceramic bowls and tiles, jewellery and Byzantine icons have been carefully produced, using original craft techniques where possible.

Following pages *View over Plaka from Acropolis towards Lykavittos Hill*

Kerameikos

Ancient Athens' outer walls run through Kerameikos, once the edge of the Classical city. It was a settlement of potters, where the distinctive red-and-black Attic vases were produced. It was from Kerameikos that the processions of the Eleusinian Mysteries began, starting from the Sacred Gate and proceeding along the Sacred Way. Perikles also delivered the famous Funeral Oration for the soldiers who died in the Peloponnesian War from the Kerameikos cemetery.

1 Pompeiion

The Pompeiion **(right)** was used to prepare for festive and religious processions, especially the annual Panathenaic procession, in which a new garment was brought to the statue of Athena in the Parthenon.

2 City Walls

The walls, which surrounded the entire city, were built by Athenian ruler Themistokles between 487 and 479 BCE. They incorporated materials from all over the city, including marble from tombs, temples and houses.

3 Sacred Gate

Through this well-preserved gate **(above)** passed the Sacred Way, reserved for pilgrims and priestesses during the procession to Eleusis *(see p115)*. A great marble sphinx was built into the gate.

4 Dipylon

The main roads from Thebes, Corinth and the Peloponnese converged at this entrance gate to Athens, the largest in ancient Greece. Many ceremonial events were held here to mark arrivals and departures.

5 Marble Bull

The bull of the tomb of Dionysios of Kollytos from 4th century BCE **(below)** is the most recognizable monument here. Its inscriptions show Dionysios was praised for his goodness, and died unmarried, mourned by his mother and sisters.

6 Sanctuary of the Tritopatores

It is uncertain who exactly the Tritopatores were, but they may have been representatives of the souls of the dead, and worshipped in an ancestor cult.

Kerameikos Site Plan

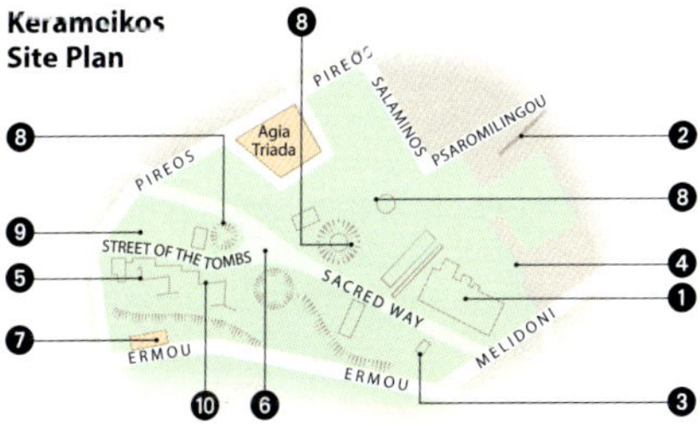

THE OLD POTTERS' DISTRICT

The name Kerameikos comes from Keramos, the patron god of ceramics. According to Pausanias *(see p51)* and other early writers, the name recalls an age-old group of potters' workshops that used to be located on the grassy banks of the river Eridanos, which cuts through the site. The museum contains fine examples of Greek urns and other pottery found at the site.

NEED TO KNOW

MAP A3–4
■ Ermou 148, Thisio
■ 210 34 63 552

Open summer: 8am–8pm daily; winter: 8:30am–3pm daily; last entry: 30 minutes before closing

Adm €10 summer, €5 winter

■ **The verdant site of Kerameikos and the surrounding industrial buildings are at their most striking in the early evening, when they are tinged pink by the setting sun.**

■ **There are several reasonably priced tavernas lining the nearby streets of Apostolou Pavlou and Eptahalkou that serve a range of traditional Greek dishes. Head to either for a hearty outdoor lunch.**

7 Kerameikos Museum

This site **(above)** is packed with fascinating finds, such as originals of many tombs replaced by casts and pottery shards of erotic scenes from a brothel.

8 Warriors' Tombs

The high, round burial mounds *(tumuli)* lining the sacred way date from the 7th century BCE and were probably first built to honour great warriors. Most have marble coffins and offerings at their centres, with the mounds built up around them.

9 Stele of Hegeso

This lovely grave pediment is one of the finest works of 5th-century BCE Attic art. Hegeso, the dead woman, is portrayed seated, taking a trinket from a box. The original is in the National Archaeological Museum.

10 Tomb of Dexileos

This marble-relief carved tomb **(below)** is of a young horseman who died in 394 BCE. Unlike here, the dead of ancient Greece were often depicted along with their living family, saying a final goodbye.

Byzantine and Christian Museum

At this museum, five thematic exhibitions, beginning with the Ancient World and taking us through the many centuries of Byzantium, narrate a vast and lasting legacy through dazzling displays of 15,000 artifacts and paintings.

1 Shepherd Carrying a Lamb

This 4th-century marble sculpture is also a Christian allegory with pagan roots. Though the shepherd is meant to be Christ, the image is taken directly from an Archaic sculpture found on the Acropolis of a man bringing a calf to be sacrificed to the goddess Athena.

2 Treasury of Mytilene

A collection of 6th-century silver vessels, gold jewellery and coins, discovered in a sunken ship off the island of Mytilene (Lesvos). Scholars believe the valuables were brought to the island to be hidden, and were never recovered by their owners.

3 Orpheus Playing a Lyre

Orpheus **(left)** is surrounded by animals, creating an allegory of Christ and his followers. This transmutation of ancient pagan myths into the new religion of Christianity was an essential element of Byzantine art.

5 Mosaic Icon of the Mother of God (The Episkepsis)

This 13th-century mosaic **(above)** shows the Mother of God and Child, in the pose known as *Glykophiloussa*, imploring Her Son to save the world. Mosaic icons are rare – only about 40 are known to exist – and all originate from Constantinople.

4 Precious Ecclesiastical Artifacts

This case contains a late 14th-century wooden cross covered with silver and embellished with small steatite icons, a 10th-century copper chalice, and a 14th-century silk stole decorated with holy figures embroidered in metallic and silk thread.

NEED TO KNOW

MAP P3 ■ Vasilissis Sofias 22 ■ www.byzantine museum.gr

Open 8:30am–3:30pm Wed–Mon

Adm €8; €4 winter & reduced; EU citizens between 6–25 free

■ **In summer, there are often concerts in the museum's vast courtyard. Call ahead to find out what's on and when.**

■ **There is a café-bistro, Ilissia, located in the museum garden. Stop by for a light snack and a cup of coffee. Alternatively, head to one of the tavernas in nearby, lively Pangráti district or in Kolonaki.**

8 Double-Sided Icon of St George

Large, double-sided icons were rare in Byzantium. This unusual 13th-century example **(left)** is carved in three dimensions and depicts the full body. The other side also has two female saints in relief.

> **ARISTOTLE'S LYKEIO**
>
> Building plans for a neighbouring site were shelved when ancient ruins were discovered. These were later identified as the Lykeio of Aristotle (founded to compete with Plato's Academy). The site can now be visited but little aside from the foundations remain *(open 8am–8pm daily)*.

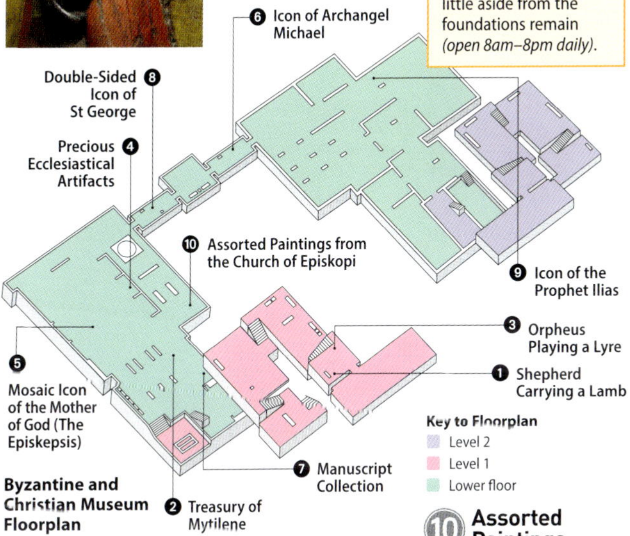

Byzantine and Christian Museum Floorplan

6 Icon of Archangel Michael

Set in a glowing field of gold, this 14th-century icon from Constantinople depicts the Archangel Michael with a sceptre and orb, symbolic of the terrestrial world.

7 Manuscript Collection

The highlight of this collection is an early 14th-century imperial *chrysobull* (edict) issued by Emperor Andronikos II Paleologos. The top of the scroll bears a miniature showing the emperor himself handing a document to Christ, while at the bottom, the emperor's signature appears in red ink.

9 Icon of the Prophet Ilias

This late 17th-century icon, titled *The Ascension of the Prophet Ilias and Scenes from his Life*, is signed by Cretan artist Theodore Poulakis. It depicts the prophet riding a flaming chariot. Elijah (Ilias in Greek), along with Jesus and the Panagia, is the only biblical character to physically ascend to heaven.

10 Assorted Paintings from the Church of Episkopi

Probably created during the 17th century, the *temblon* (icon screen) paintings **(below)** depict biblical scenes. Other paintings dating back to the 9th, 11th and 13th centuries are displayed as they would have been in the old Evrytanian church.

TOP 10 Philopappos Hill

The pine-covered slopes of Philopappos Hill offer a pleasantly shaded maze of paths leading through monuments marking centuries of history. Known as "the hill of muses" in antiquity, it has been a source of inspiration for countless poets. On the first Monday of Lent, the hill swarms with hundreds of Athenians, who gather here to fly kites.

1 The Deme of Koile

This ancient road leads from the Acropolis to Piraeus, passing between Philopappos Hill and the Pnyx to follow the course of the Long Walls (5th century BCE). It was a two-lane road, 8–12 m (26–40 ft) wide, with anti-slip grooves. A 500-m (1,600-ft) stretch has been excavated.

2 Old National Observatory

Greece's oldest research centre is housed in a beautiful Neo-Classical building. The centre monitors astronomy, weather and, especially, the earthquakes that occasionally rattle Athens.

3 Hill of the Nymphs

In ancient times, Greeks believed Philopappos was inhabited by the muses of art, music and poetry. This smaller hill was home of the nymphs – the female spirits of trees, mountain tops and springs.

4 Socrates' Prison

This is believed to be the cave **(left)** where Socrates *(see p50)* was imprisoned, having been condemned to death. His disciples sat with him as he drank the hemlock that dispatched him.

5 The Pnyx

If Athens is the cradle of democracy, this spot **(right)** is its exact birthplace. After Athens became a democracy in 508 BCE, the first ever democratic congress met here weekly, and the greatest orators held forth. The limestone theatre, cut into the hill, accommodated over 10,000.

6 Church of Agia Marina

Agia Marina **(below)** is associated with childbirth and sick children, and pregnant women used to come here and slip down a carved slide to ensure a safe delivery. In the past, mothers brought sick children here to spend the night. A colourful festival honours Marina on 16th and 17th July every year.

7 Church of Agios Dimitrios Lombardiaris

In 1648, an Ottoman commander planned to bombard this charming Byzantine church. But lightning struck his cannon, giving the church the epithet 'Lombardiaris', a corruption of Bombardier.

8 Philopappos Monument

Syrian-born prince and Roman consul, Gaius Julius Antiochus Philopappos, admired Classical Greek culture. He retired in Athens and died here in about 114 CE. The Greeks built a marble tomb and monument **(left)** after two years showing him as an Athenian citizen, surrounded by his royal Commagene family. Its partially destroyed form looks across to the Acropolis.

THE 1687 SIEGE

During an attempt to seize the Ottoman-occupied Acropolis, the Venetians garrisoned themselves on Philopappos Hill, the perfect strategic location to shell their target. Too perfect, unfortunately – one of their shells hit the Parthenon, where the Turks stored their gunpowder, and the ensuing explosion severely damaged the Acropolis's prized temple and sculptures.

9 Hilltop View

You may not feel that you deserve such a jaw-dropping view after such an easy, shaded walk. But the hilltop directly overlooks the Acropolis and all of southern Athens stretching to the sea. This was once a favourite vantage-point for generals – and it's equally appealing to photographers today.

NEED TO KNOW

MAP B6 ■ Enter from Dionysiou Areopagitou

Dora Stratou Dance Theatre: **MAP C5** ■ Performances: May–late Sep: 9:30pm Thu & Fri, 8:30pm Sat & Sun, call to confirm. Tickets from the theatre, or call 2103 244 395 ■ Adm €30; children €10 ■ www.grdance.org

■ **Though perfectly safe during the day, the unlit paths of Philopappos Hill are best avoided after dark.**

■ **Cafés along Apostolou Pavlou, north of the Dionysiou Aeropagitou entrance to Philopappos Hill, offer refreshments with fine views – albeit often at higher prices. On the west lies Petralona district, full of good-value tavernas.**

10 Dora Stratou Dance Theatre

In 1953, Dora Stratou founded a dance troupe which toured Greece, learning hundreds of endangered regional dances that preserve Greek culture. The troupe still presents the intricate steps.

Philoppapos Hill Map

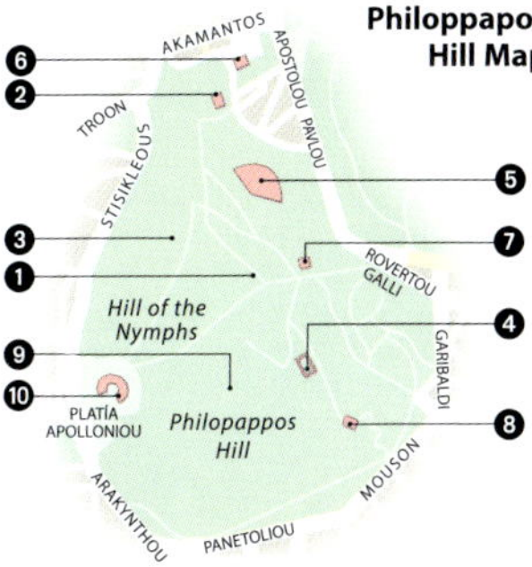

Temple of Olympian Zeus

The majestic temple to the ruler of the pantheon was the largest on mainland Greece. Inside stood two colossal statues: one of the god in gold and ivory, and one of the Roman Emperor Hadrian. Though the temple's construction began in 515 BCE, political turmoil delayed its completion for nearly 700 years. To thank Hadrian for finishing it, in 131 CE the Athenians built a two-storey arch next to the temple, whose inscription announces Hadrian's claim on the city.

1 Valerian Wall

Enclosing several buildings within the temple complex was a wall **(below)** commissioned by the Roman emperor Valerian in the 3rd century CE. Many of the temples it surrounded were demolished to provide marble for the wall.

WHY DID IT TAKE SO LONG TO BUILD?

The tyrant Peisistratos started the Temple of Olympian Zeus in 515 BCE to keep the rebellious Athenians occupied. After his fall in 510 BCE, the work ceased. In 175 BCE, Syrian king Antiochos IV of Epiphanes resumed the construction work, but it stopped with his death in 164 BC. Finally, Emperor Hadrian (ruled 117–138 CE) overlooked the completion of the temple and also personally consecrated it in 31–132 CE.

2 Temple of Olympian Zeus

Zeus had long been worshipped on this site, and there was at least one other temple to him before this one. Sixteen magnificent columns **(above)** survive from the original 104.

Hadrian's Arch 3

Emperor Hadrian had the west side of this arch **(right)** inscribed "This is Athens, the ancient city of Theseus", and the east side "This is the city of Hadrian and not of Theseus", distinguishing the cities of ancient legend and Roman reality.

4 Themistoklean Gates

Around the site are remains of the wall built by political leader Themistokles in 479 BCE, to defend Athens from continuing onslaughts by the Persians.

5 Law Court at the Delphinion

Now mostly in ruins, this law court, from 500 BCE, is thought to be on the site of the palace of mythical king Aegeas, the father of Theseus *(see p53)*.

9 Roman Baths

Among the many ruins of "Hadrianopolis", the first structures of Hadrian's new city, are these foundations **(above)**, actually the best-preserved Roman bath house in Athens. It once had a coloured mosaic floor.

10 Temple of Apollo Delphinios and Artemis Delphinia

The temple was built to honour the god-and-goddess siblings Apollo and Artemis, celebrating them in the form of two dolphins.

NEED TO KNOW

MAP L5 ■ Leoforos Vas. Olgas 1 at Amalias ■ www.odysseus.culture.gr

Open summer: 8am–8pm daily (winter: to 3pm; shoulder season: hours vary, check website)

Adm: €20 summer, €10 reduced and winter

■ **To get the best light for photographs, come in the late afternoon.**

■ **For a tasty meal head across Vassilisis Olgas to Aegli Café-Bistro by the Zappeion, or across Leoforos Syngrou to one of the many tavernas around Platia Tsokri.**

6 Ruins of Houses

Ancient pipes, foundations and domestic objects show that people lived and built houses here between the 5th century BCE and 2nd century CE – the whole time it took to build the temple.

7 Temple of Kronos and Rhea

This temple to Zeus's parents was built in the 5th century BCE; now only the foundations remain. Rhea saved Zeus from Kronos, then Zeus took dominion of the universe as ruler of the gods.

8 Temple of Zeus Panhellenios

Hadrian promoted the cult of Zeus Panhellenios ("ruler of all the Greeks") and associated himself with the god. Offers to god and emperor were made in this temple, later demolished for the Valerian wall.

Temple of Olympian Zeus Map

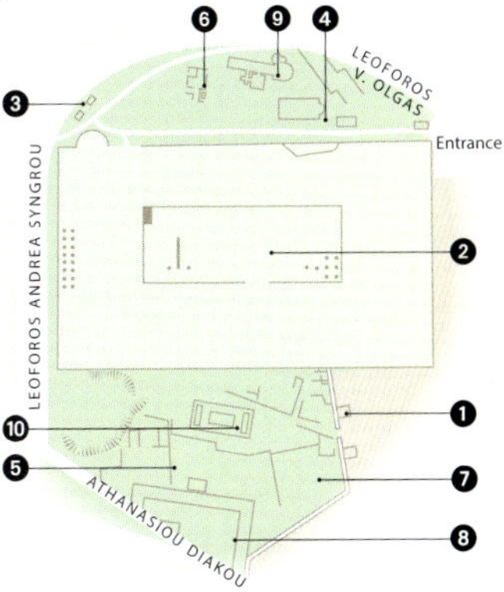

The Top 10 of Everything

Archaeological display at the Acropolis Museum, Athens

TOP 10 Moments in History

1 Birth of Athens

The Acropolis was first inhabited in Neolithic times (around 3000 BCE), and began to take on the form of a city when it was fortified by the Mycenaeans (inhabitants of the southeastern Greek mainland) in about 1400 BCE.

2 Golden Age

The city-state developed into a colonial power in the 6th and 5th centuries BCE. Under Perikles (495–429 BCE) Athens enjoyed its greatest period of building, when the Parthenon, Erechtheion and Temple of Nike were erected. Cultural life flourished until Sparta's defeat of Athens in the Peloponnesian War (431–404 BCE).

Bust of the Greek statesman Perikles

3 Roman Athens

Roman rule began in 146 BCE and lasted five centuries. Athenians initially maintained good relations with their rulers, but in 86 BCE Athens sided with rebel King Mithridates of Pontos and was sacked by Sulla. Emperor Hadrian (76–138 CE) remained a great admirer of Greek culture, however, and finished the Greek Zeus sanctuary. Later, in about 150 CE, Herode Atticus funded the great theatre *(see p13)* that bears his name.

4 Byzantine Period

In 395 CE, when Roman territory was divided, Greece fell within the Eastern Empire, then became part of the Byzantine Empire. By 389–393 CE, philosophical schools were closed, pagan temples converted to churches and the Olympic Games suspended.

5 Ottoman Athens

The Ottoman Turks took Athens in 1456 from the Latin Catholic dukes, and the city became a provincial backwater. After bombarding the Parthenon, the Venetians held the city briefly in 1687. A few decades later, English and French artists began visiting Athens as part of the Grand Tour, aiding its rebirth, but also pilfering ancient artworks.

6 War of Independence

In 1821 Greeks rose against Ottoman domination – first alone, then with the aid of Britain, France and Russia. The war ended in 1829, but the Ottomans held the Acropolis until 1834, when King Otto I entered the city. Athens became capital of the new Greek state and was rebuilt, largely in Neo-Classical style.

Painting of the War of Independence

7 World War II

Mussolini declared war on Greece in October 1940, and the German army entered Athens on 23 April 1941, raising the swastika over the Acropolis. The Third Reich used the Hotel Grande Bretagne *(see p144)* as its wartime headquarters.

German planes during World War II

8 Post World War II

Greece fell into civil war in 1946, with the US began pouring economic and military aid into the country to prevent the Communist rebels from taking power. In the 1950s and 1980s, Athens saw rapid industrialization, mass migration from rural areas and growth of sprawling suburbs.

9 Military Dictatorship

On 21 April 1967, a coup d'état led by Georgios Papadopoulos marked the beginning of a seven-year military junta. Student protests during mid-November 1973 were violently suppressed by the military, who stormed Athens' Polytechnic, killing many. The junta fell in July 1974.

10 Modern-Day Athens

Greece joined the EEC (now the EU) in 1981. In 1985, Athens was the first European Capital of Culture. The 2004 Olympics gave the city improved transport, sports and cultural facilities. In 2010, however, economic crisis led to almost a decade of social unrest. Severe wildfires have occurred in and around Athens, adding further challenges. Tourism is on a steady rise, which has an overall positive impact on the economy but puts a strain on local infrastructure and resources.

TOP 10 ATHENIANS

1 Draco
In the 7th century BCE, Draco instituted the first Code of Law: even trivial crimes incurred the death penalty, hence the term draconian.

2 Solon
Draco's laws were made less severe by Solon (c.638–559 BCE). He also extended citizenship to the lower classes.

3 Kleisthenes
A statesman active around 508–506 BCE, Kleisthenes replaced aristocratic rule with a democratic Assembly.

4 Themistokles
This general (c.524–459 BCE) championed the navy as a force to expand the empire.

5 Perikles
Perikles (c.495–429 BCE) beautified the city, let poorer citizens attend the Assembly, and extended the empire.

6 Aspasia
The consort of Perikles, Aspasia, was famed for her intellect and regarded as one of the most influential women in Athenian society during the 5th century BCE.

7 Lela Karagianni
Karagianni (1898–1944), a resistance leader during World War II, was executed weeks before Athens' liberation.

8 Damaskinos
Archbishop of Athens from 1941, he defied the Nazi occupiers by issuing false baptismal certificates for Jews.

9 Dimitris Pikionis
Distinguished architect (1887–1968) who designed the 1950s stone walkways on the Acropolis' south slope.

10 Melina Mercouri
Much-loved actress (1920–94) who opposed the 1967–74 junta, became Minister of Culture and initiated the European Capital of Culture scheme.

The actress Melina Mercouri

TOP 10 Moments in the History of Theatre and Music

A modern production of *The Persians*, a play by Aeschylus

1 The Rites of Dionysos, 1200–600 BCE

Annual rites to the god of wine and revelry were held each spring, and involved orgies, feasts and the ingestion of herbs that led to wild ecstasies. A dithyramb (ode to Dionysos) was sung by a chorus of men dressed as satyrs. It eventually evolved into narratives, which in turn developed into the first plays.

2 Thespis, 6th Century BCE

During one of these group chorales, an intrepid performer named Thespis broke away from the group and added a solo narrative. The innovation took hold, and this new individual role became known as the protagonist, the individual hero of the drama, now backed by the chorus.

3 Drama Competitions, 534 BCE

In 534 BCE, the ruler of Athens, Peisistratos, formalized the Dionysian festivals into fully fledged drama competitions, held annually. Thespis won the first competition.

4 Aeschylus, the First Playwright, 472 BCE

Aeschylus introduced a second character, the antagonist, creating new possibilities. In 472 BC came *The Persians*, the earliest known play.

5 Sophocles Beats Aeschylus in the Drama Competition, 468 BCE

Sophocles brought another innovation to the form of drama: a third character. He also wrote what is still considered one of the greatest masterpieces of tragedy, *Oedipus Rex*.

Greek shadow puppet

6 Greek Shadow Puppet Theatre, 16th Century

After the peak of Athenian drama, Greece's performing arts stagnated. However, during the Ottoman occupation, Greeks drew on an Eastern tradition of shadow puppet theatre. The stylized spectacles were satirical and bawdy, the main character (the cunning Karaghiozis) joking at the expense of his social betters.

7 Rembetika Emerges, 1920s

With the arrival of Greek refugees from Asia Minor, a unique and now beloved genre developed. Based on distinctive eastern musical modes and played often on the bouzouki and baglamas, rembetika is urban Greek blues. Its lyrics evoke the themes of hard luck and troubled times.

8 Maria Callas Dominates Opera, 1950s and 1960s

Greece's illustrious diva mesmerized millions with her definitive performances on the world's greatest stages. Her life off stage, including her much publicized relationship with Aristotle Onasis, was equally rich in drama and passion.

9 Mikis Theodorakis Writes the Songs of a Generation, 1960s and 1970s

Mikis Theodorakis, Greece's greatest modern composer, won international acclaim with works such as *Epiphania* and the instantly recognizable *Zorba the Greek* score. During the junta, Theodorakis's songs were banned and he was jailed, making him an instant symbol of the resistance.

Iconic composer Mikis Theodorakis

10 The Opening Ceremony for the Athens Olympic Games, 2004

Dimitris Papapioannou's lyrical voyage through the history of Greece and the journey of mankind featured a poem by Nobel laureate Giorgos Seferis, stunning costumes by Sophia Kokosalaki, and a performance by Bjork.

TOP 10 THEATRE AND MUSIC VENUES

The National Opera

1 National Opera
A state-of-the-art theatre hosting ballet, opera and experimental projects *(see p111)*.

2 Gazi Technopolis
MAP A3 ■ Piraeus St 100 ■ www.athens-technopolis.gr
The industrial complex of the historic gasworks is now one of Athens' finest outdoor venues.

3 Onassis Stegi
MAP T2 ■ Leof Andrea Siggrou 107
A spectacular 880-seat amphitheatre hosting performances of all kinds.

4 National Theatre
Catch the National Theatre's classic performances here *(see p96)*.

5 Kyttaro
MAP C1 ■ Acharnon at Ipeirou
One of Athens' best live stages for rock and metal.

6 Gagarin 205
MAP B1 ■ Liosion 205, Attiki metro ■ 211 411 2500 ■ www.gagarin25.gr
Great musicians often play at this venue.

7 Megaro Mousikis
MAP G3 ■ Vas Sofias and Kokkali ■ www.megaro.gr
Acoustics for the world's best orchestras, jazz bands and ballet companies.

8 Lykavittos Theatre
MAP F2 ■ 210 722 7233
This theatre showcases the best musical acts, from rock to classical.

9 Half Note
MAP M6 ■ Trivonianou 17 ■ www.halfnote.gr
Top-notch jazz musicians play here.

10 Epidauros
Only ancient classics are performed in this famous amphitheatre *(see p125)*. Tickets are available from the Herodes Atticus or Panepistimiou box offices.

TOP 10 Archaeological Sites

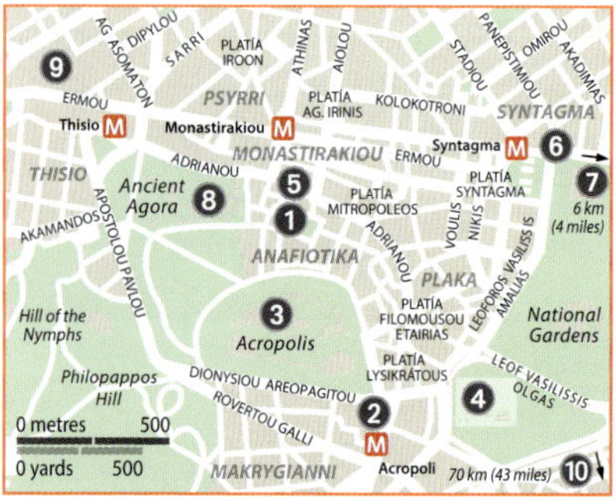

1 Roman Forum and Tower of the Winds

One of the city's most interestingly layered sites *(see pp24–5)*. Buildings and ruins include the ingenious Tower of the Winds from 50 BCE, the 1st-century CE Roman forum, and a well-restored Ottoman mosque.

The Tower of the Winds

2 Acropolis Museum

The museum *(see pp14–15)* has been built over a late-Roman and early Byzantine settlement. The site is packed with houses and at least one fountain and reservoir, rare in the parched city. A walkway through the site and glass floors in the museum allow visitors to see all angles of it, a fascinating juxtaposition to the earlier archaeological finds within the museum *(see p77)*.

3 Acropolis

If you're only in Athens for a day, this is the one sight to see *(see pp12–13)*. The temples, especially the great Parthenon, built to honour Athena, have been a dominating influence in Western architecture for over 2,000 years. They continue to astonish and inspire.

4 Temple of Olympian Zeus

The building of the colossal temple to Zeus *(see pp36–7)* was started in 515 BCE and took nearly 700 years to complete, during which time many other buildings – temples, baths and a law court – sprang up around it.

5 Hadrian's Library

Hadrian built this luxurious Corinthian-columned building *(see p84)* in 132 CE. Most of the space was a showy marble courtyard, with gardens and a pool. There were also lecture rooms, music rooms and a theatre. The library itself was on the east side, where you can see marble slots for manuscript scrolls.

6 Syntagma Metro Station

In the late 1990s, Athens undertook its biggest archaeological dig ever: excavating a long-delayed metro *(see p101)* – essential for hosting the Olympics. Many feared that the tightly scheduled dig would endanger what lay beneath. The Syntagma metro station was a brilliant compromise: though modern and gleaming, one glass wall looks directly through to an archaeological site, with detailed explanations of its various layers.

Kesariani monastery

7 Kesariani

MAP T2 ■ 210 723 6619 ■ Open 8:30am–3pm Wed–Mon ■ Adm

This 11th-century monastery on the cypress-clad slopes of Mount Ymittos (the ancient Hymettos) makes a wonderful day trip (best reached by car). The chapel, dedicated to the Presentation of the Theotokos, is built atop Classical ruins, and its walls are decorated with cloisonné (enamelled) masonry and late 17th-century paintings. The ram's-head fountain is said to cure infertility.

8 Ancient Agora

The Ancient Agora *(see pp16–17)*, the marketplace where philosophers held forth, tradesmen bickered and statesmen hammered out the terms of the first democracy, was the city's heart and soul for 1200 years. This is one of the most hands-on sites in Athens and includes the Temple of Hephaistos, the best-preserved ancient Greek temple.

9 Kerameikos

This fascinating site *(see pp30–31)* around ancient Athens' walls should not be missed. It contains evidence of all the activities that take place at a city's edge: tombs (raised circular mounds for war heroes, pompous marble statues for great statesmen), temples, important roads, pottery workshops and a brothel. It's also a shady oasis in the congested city centre.

10 Temple of Poseidon

Located 70 km (43 miles) south of Athens is a great marble shrine *(see p130)* to the sea god, Poseidon. Poised on Cape Sounio's summit and surrounded by the Aegean Sea, this temple is among the most stunning sights in all of Greece. It was built in the early 5th century BCE but captivated imaginations for centuries thereafter. British poet Lord Byron was one of many who fell under its spell, composing poetry in its honour and carving his name on a pillar some 2,400 years later. Come at sunset, just before it closes, for unforgettable views.

Temple of Poseidon at Cape Sounio

TOP 10 Churches

1 Church of the Metamorphosis (Sotiros)

MAP C5 ■ Theorias St, Upper Plaka

This Byzantine church is situated on the northern slope of the Acropolis and dates back either to the second half of the 11th century or the 14th century. It is a four-columned church with a tall Athenian dome, typical of monuments from this period. The dome and the northern and southern sides have remained intact, but the western sides have been rebuilt.

2 Monastiraki

Once the greatest monastery of the area *(see p86)*, this is the church from which the Monastiraki neighbourhood takes its name. "Little monastery" was so called after the destruction of its many surrounding buildings during 19th-century archaeological digs. The restored church itself is usually open.

3 Kesariani, Mount Ymittos

This 11th-century monastery *(see p45)* sits on fragrant, wooded slopes just outside Athens. Most of its surviving frescoes are from the 16th and 17th centuries, and its fountain waters that were said to cure infertility, are no longer drinkable.

4 Agii Apostoli

MAP J4

The Church of the Holy Apostles is one of Athens' oldest churches, built in the early 11th century over a 2nd-century monument in the Ancient Agora. Though it suffered a great deal of damage during the Ottoman occupation, the remains of its frescoes have been preserved and restored within.

The 11th-century church, Agii Apostoli

Interior of Kapnikarea

5 Kapnikarea

This lovely little church *(see p87)*, dedicated to the Presentation of the Theotokos, was built in the 11th century over the ruins of an ancient temple. It is laid out in the typical Byzantine cross-in-square plan, with three apses on the east side and a narthex (a western portico). Inside, the church is decorated with frescoes by neo-Byzantinist Photis Kontoglou.

6 Panagia Grigoroussa/ Agios Fanourios

MAP J4 ■ Near Monastiraki Metro Station ■ Services: Apr–Oct: 5:45pm Sat; Nov–Mar: 4:45pm Sat

If you've lost something, head to this church. Fanourios is the patron saint of lost objects. Every Saturday, the church conducts a liturgy blessing parishioners' *fanouropites* (cakes). Once eaten, it is believed that the lost object would reappear.

7 Agios Georgios

MAP P1

Claiming the highest point in modern-day Athens – the peak of Lykavittos Hill – Agios Georgios provides stunning views as far as the Saronic Gulf, the island of Egina and the Peloponnese coast. Services are held both inside and outside.

8 Panagia Gorgoepikoös

Dwarfed by the bulk of the modern Mitropoli, tiny Panagia Gorgoepikoös (Mikri Mitropoli, "little Cathedral", *see p79*) far outshadows its vast neighbour in historic and artistic importance. It was built in the 12th century, on the ruins of an ancient temple dedicated to goddess Eileithyia. Its walls are built of Hellentistic, Roman and Byzantine marble relics, sculpted with reliefs depicting the ancient calendar of feasts.

9 Agia Ekaterini

Fragments of Classical columns remain in the courtyard of this beautiful 12th-century church *(see p80)*. It was built over the ruins of an ancient temple, possibly dedicated to the goddess Hestia. The church's colourful frescoes have been lovingly restored.

Religious art in Mitropoli

10 Mitropoli

Athens' massive Metropolitan Cathedral *(see p79)* of 1862 was the first major church built after Greece's independence. It became the seat of the archbishop and hence of the established Greek state church. Though its colourful frescoes and pricey ecclesiastical objects are certainly impressive, its architecture is less so. Mitropoli's importance is almost entirely spiritual, as the focal point for the Greek Orthodox Church.

TOP 10 Museums

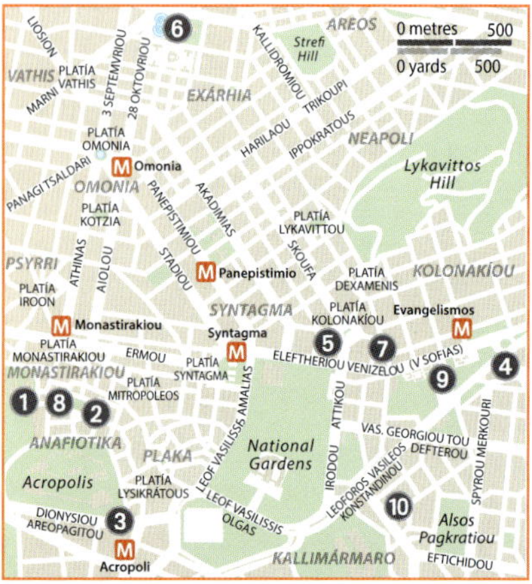

1 Agora Museum

The fascinating displays of finds *(see pp18–19)* from the city's ancient marketplace focus on objects used in the workings of the first democracy, including the declaration inscribed on marble that a government of democracy, not tyranny, was to rule.

2 Museum of Greek Musical Instruments

Greek musical instruments are far more varied than the bouzouki that plucked out the theme to *Zorba the Greek*. The Greek musical tradition, though heavily influenced by Turkey and the Middle East, has been filtered through the unique Hellenic sensibility. The array of beautiful instruments includes carved Byzantine lyres, ivory-inlaid lutes and pastoral flutes *(see p78)*.

3 Acropolis Museum

This beautiful museum *(see pp14–15)* was designed partly to provide a fitting home for the famed marble sculptures of the Acropolis. The collection of sculptures arranged within the orientation and dimensions of the Parthenon can be seen from the glass walls on the top floor.

4 National Gallery of Art

Vassileos Konstantinou 50 ■ Open 10am–9pm Wed, 10am–6pm Thu–Mon ■ Adm ■ www.nationalgallery.gr

Greece's most important art gallery showcases the masterpieces of Greek artists. Highlights include works by avant-garde contemporary artist Chryssa, the Neo-Byzantinist Photis Kontoglou and the Expressionist Sophia Laskaridou, as well as 19th-century masters such as Nikiforos Lytras and Theodoros Vryzakis.

Display of lutes at the Museum of Greek Musical Instruments

5 Benaki Museum of Greek Culture

Follow the progress of Greek art and culture through this first-rate collection from the eras of antiquity to the mid-20th century. Walk through excellently presented displays in the gorgeous Neo-Classical mansion *(see pp26–7)* of the Benaki family.

Bishop's hat, Benaki Museum of Greek Culture

6 National Archaeological Museum

One of the world's most important museums *(see pp20–21)*, featuring an array of treasures from the prehistoric and Classical Greek civilizations. Don't miss the exquisite frescoes of 17th-century-BCE Thera, and the golden hoard of Bronze Age Mycenae.

National Archaeological Museum

7 Museum of Cycladic Art

The Cycladic island civilization of the Aegean produced something very different: strangely elegant, stylized marble goddess-cult figurines *(see p102)*. These were the first pieces in the centuries-long tradition of Greek art that was to follow and this is the world's largest collection *(see pp22–3)*.

8 Museum of Modern Greek Culture

Areos 10 ■ Open 9:30am–4:30pm Mon & Thu, 8am–8pm Wed & Fri–Sun ■ www.mnep.gr

Set in a complex of 18 historic buildings, this museum showcases Greece's cultural heritage with displays on textile design, traditional dress, shadow puppetry and other folk arts, as well as exhibits on the cosmopolitan life of modern Athens. A short film gives an overview of the eventful decades since the founding of the country. All displays have explanations in English.

9 The Basil and Elise Goulandris Foundation

This outstanding collection *(see p103)* is the newest star on the Athens museum circuit. Fine works by Miro, van Gogh, Picasso, Monet, Cezanne, Kiefer, Lichtenstein, and many other late 19th and 20th century artists, are joined by pieces by modern Greek artists of international renown, including Takis, Moralis, Tsarouchis, Parthenis and Ghika. Guided tours in English are on Sundays at 10am.

10 Byzantine and Christian Museum

Yet another of the top museums in the world *(see pp32–3)*. There are nearly 30,000 objects from Byzantine and post-Byzantine churches and monasteries across Greece, including sculpture, manuscripts, icons, frescoes and precious, eye-strainingly intricate gold, silver and gem-encrusted ecclesiastical objects.

Exhibits at the Byzantine and Christian Museum

TOP 10 Philosophers and Writers

1 Homer c.700 BCE

Next to nothing is known about the bard who compiled the tales of *The Iliad* and *The Odyssey*. These poems, which were kept alive by oral tradition, are arguably the greatest and most influential in history.

Homer

2 Sappho 630–570 BCE

One of the finest poets of ancient Greece – Plato called her "the Tenth Muse" – Sappho is known for natural and spontaneous style. Themes of love, longing and passion, often for women, have long associated her with lesbian love, and the word lesbian is in fact derived from Sappho's home, the island of Lesbos.

3 Sophocles 496–406 BCE

Only seven of Sophocles' plays survive, but his reputation rests securely on three: *Antigone*, *Oedipus at Kolonos* and *Oedipus Rex*. The last of these, the story of a king bound hopelessly by fate to murder his father and marry his mother, is considered the greatest masterpiece of Greek tragedy.

4 Socrates 470–399 BCE

Though Socrates himself wrote nothing, his teachings, recorded in the writings of historians and especially his pupil Plato, have earned him the title of the forerunner of Western philosophy. At the height of the Golden Age of Athens, the original marketplace philosopher debated the great meanings in the Ancient Agora, and was eventually tried and put to death *(see p34)* for corrupting the youth of Athens.

5 Aristophanes 447–385 BCE

The greatest comic playwright of Greece brought a welcome breath of fresh air and levity after the age of the great tragedians. Aristophanes' raunchy, hilarious *Lysistrata*, in which the women of warring Sparta and Athens refuse to sleep with their husbands until they stop fighting, remains one of the greatest anti-war messages of all time.

6 Plato 428–348 BCE

If Socrates was the forerunner of Western philosophy, then Plato was its foundation. His works – from his early dialogues reprising Socrates' teachings, to later masterworks such as the seminal *Republic* – comprised the backbone of every major intellectual movement to follow.

Plato and Aristotle, as portrayed by Raphael in *The School of Athens*

7 Aristotle 384–322 BCE

After studying with Plato, Aristotle tutored Alexander the Great. He later set up the Lykeio, a competitor to Plato's Academy. His *Poetics* is still one of the most

Aristotle tutoring Alexander the Great

important works of literary criticism, and his *Nichomachean Ethics* is among the greatest treatises on ethics.

8 Nikos Kazantzakis 1883–1957

Many have been drawn to the strange, joyous, bittersweet spirit of modern Greece, as depicted in Kazantzakis' most famous work, *Zorba the Greek*. Darker in mood is *The Last Temptation of Christ*, and best of all is his autobiographical *Report to Greco*, which among other things chronicles his childhood in Ottoman Crete.

9 George Seferis 1900–71

Greece's first Nobel Laureate was born in Smyrna, which fell to modern Turkey in 1922, and his lyrical poetry is inspired by history and feelings of exile. His work also relates Greece's Classical past to its raw present, as in *Mythistorema*, a series of poems that draws from *The Odyssey*.

10 Katerina Anghelaki-Rooke 1939–2020

One of the most notable and loved poets of modern Greece, Anghelaki-Rooke began her career at just 17, with the encouragement of her godfather, Nikos Kazantzakis. Her philosophical, sensual poetry explores the limitations and triumphs of the body, and the essential nature of passion.

TOP 10 TOMES

1 *The Iliad*, Homer
One small episode in the Trojan War, told in the greatest epic ever written.

2 *The Odyssey*, Homer
Detailing Odysseus's adventures with sirens, nymphs and Kyklops as he makes his way from Troy back home to the island of Ithaca.

3 *The Oresteia*, Aeschylus
Brilliant trilogy about the House of Atreus, the most dysfunctional family in ancient Greece.

4 *The Theban Tragedies*, Sophocles
Terrible events unfold when Oedipus kills his father and marries his mother. A dramatic text to read on a visit to Delphi and Thebes.

5 *The Republic*, Plato
Pluto's celebrated work remains the blueprint for how to effectively run a government.

6 *Constitution of Athens*, Aristotle
A work that marries the political structure of Athens with the architectural structure of the Ancient Agora.

7 *History of the Peloponnesian War*, Thucydides
Month-by-month, blow-by-blow historical account of the conflict by an Athenian officer.

8 *The Histories*, Herodotus
Compelling reportage of the Greeks' fight for freedom against the Persians, as told by the "Father of History".

9 *The Guide to Greece*, Pausanias
Pausanias, arguably the world's first travel writer, recorded observations from all over Greece during his 2nd-century CE journey.

10 *Zorba the Greek*, Nikos Kazantzakis
Rose to fame as a modern Greek novel after a film adaptation was made in 1964.

Anthony Quinn in *Zorba the Greek*

Top 10 Athenian Legends

Painting depicting the story of Theseus killing the Minotaur

1 Theseus Kills the Minotaur

Upon the death of his son in Athens, Minos, King of Crete, demanded the King of Athens, Aegeas, send regular tributes of 14 youths and maidens, who were sacrificed to the monstrous Minotaur. One year, Theseus was sent and, with the help of Minos's daughter, Ariadne, he killed the Minotaur, saving hundreds of future Athenians.

2 The Birth of Erichthonios

Hephaistos tried to rape Athena, but only managed to spill his seed on her leg. Athena brushed it to the ground, where it turned into an infant with the help of the earth-goddess Gaia. Athena entrusted the daughters of King Kekrops to raise the child. After he grew up Erichthonios assumed the throne.

The Birth of Erichthonios

3 The Birth of Athena

Zeus was told that his pregnant mistress Metis would have a son who would dethrone him. To prevent this, he swallowed Metis, but the unborn child continued to grow in Zeus's head. After nine months, Hephaistos split open the god's head with an axe, and out sprang the fully grown goddess Athena, in complete armour.

4 The Naming of Athens

Athena and Poseidon, god of the sea, competed for patronage of the city by offering useful gifts. Poseidon struck his trident into the rock of the Acropolis and out gushed salt water. Athena offered the olive tree, and the city was awarded to her.

5 Theseus's Arrival in Athens

Theseus, son of King Aegeas, was raised far from court in Troezen. At 16, wielding his father's sword, Theseus left for Athens, en route slaying six bandits or monsters terrorizing Attica. He became Athens' greatest king.

6 The Abduction of Persephone

When Persephone (daughter of Demeter, the goddess of fertility and agriculture) was abducted by Hades, the earth withered. Zeus intervened, but Hades induced Persephone to eat a pomegranate, ensuring her yearly return – a divine explanation for the seasons and the cycle of rebirth.

7 The Trial of Orestes

After murdering his mother, Klytemnestra (to avenge her murder of his father, Agamemnon), Orestes was pursued to Athens by the Furies (goddesses of vengeance). Athena decreed that, instead of being killed, Orestes should stand trial. The trial marked a turning point in Athens, from blood feuds to rule of law.

8 Athena and Arachne

As goddess of spinning, Athena decided to help a poor but talented weaver called Arachne. Arachne won great admiration but never credited the goddess, so Athena challenged her to a weaving contest. Arachne's work depicted the inappropriate love affairs of the gods; Athena, indignant at this disrespect, turned Arachne into the first spider.

A portrait of Arachne weaving

9 The Death of Aegeas

Theseus had told his father that if he succeeded in killing the Minotaur, he would change his ship's sails from black to white. But, after all the excitement, he forgot. Upon seeing the black sails, Aegeas was stricken with grief and plunged to his death in the sea (now the Aegean).

10 Perseus Kills Medusa

Perseus was the son of Zeus and the maiden Danae. The king of Seriphos, Polydektes desired Danae, but Perseus promised him the snake-infested head of Medusa in exchange for his mother's safety. Perseus slew Medusa with Athena's help, then turned Polydektes to stone.

TOP 10 GODS AND MONSTERS

1 Zeus
The Pantheon's supreme god ruled the skies and fathered hundreds of heroes with his superhuman libido.

2 Poseidon
The god of the sea was Zeus's brother – and sometimes his greatest rival.

3 Athena
Zeus's daughter was a virgin warrior goddess of wisdom and crafts. She was also goddess of weaving and patron of Athens.

4 Medusa
The gaze of this snake-headed gorgon turned men to stone. In ancient Greek art, she was considered apotropaic, and used to ward off evil spirits.

5 Artemis
Apollo's twin sister was goddess of the moon, wild animals and the hunt, and remained a virgin.

6 Aphrodite
Voluptuous Aphrodite was Artemis's polar opposite – the temperamental goddess of love had dozens of affairs.

7 The Minotaur
Crete's Queen Pasiphae conceived this bull-headed, human-bodied monster with a bull sent by Poseidon.

8 The Kykopes
The most famous of these one-eyed giants is Polyphemos, the monstrous son of Poseidon whom Odysseus blinded in Homer's *The Odyssey*.

9 The Sirens
The beautiful sirens with their bewitching songs nearly lured Odysseus's sailors to their deaths on a rocky shore.

10 Apollo
The handsome god of music and poetry presided over the Muses.

Statue of the god Apollo

TOP 10 Greek Inventions

The archaeological site at Olympia

1 Olympic Games

The first recorded games were staged on the plains of Olympia in 776 BCE. Dedicated to Zeus, they lasted one day and featured running and wrestling. In 648 BCE – with the addition of boxing, the *pankration* (another form of hand-to-hand combat), horse racing and the pentathlon (sprinting, long-jump, javelin, discus and wrestling) – the event was extended to five days and held every four years.

2 Athenian Trireme

Masterpieces of ancient shipbuilding (700–400 BCE), triremes were the key to Athens' naval strength. Approximately 40 m (130 ft) long and 5 m (16 ft) wide, they were noted for great speed – up to 12 knots. The boats were powered by 170 oarsmen seated on three tiers. Only one tier rowed at a time, alternating short shifts so that they did not exhaust themselves all at once. The vessels were also equipped with sails, which were lowered during battle.

3 Theatre

The earliest form of theatre can be traced back to an ancient Greek pagan ritual, which developed into an annual drama competition in the 6th century BCE *(see p42)*. Plays were performed outside in daylight in purpose-built amphitheatres, and actors wore a range of masks to indicate different characters. The oldest plays emphasize values such as Greek patriotism, reverence to the gods, liberty and hospitality.

4 Pythagoras's Theorem

"The square of the hypotenuse of a right-angled triangle is equal to the sum of the squares of the other two sides." This theorem, discovered by the philosopher and mathematician Pythagoras (570–495 BCE) was a major scientific breakthrough, which led to extraordinary advances in mathematics, geometry and astronomy.

5 Democracy

Demokratia ("rule of the people") as a form of government was first introduced in Athens under Kleisthenes in 508–506 BCE. All free, male, adult citizens of Athenian birth were entitled to attend the Assembly – which met on the Pnyx Hill – and thus participate in political decision-making. The Assembly gathered about 40 times a year, and 6,000 citizens needed to be present to make a vote valid.

6 Hippocratic Oath

Attributed to Hippocrates, the Greek physician and the father of medicine (460–375 BCE), this oath prohibits doctors from performing unnecessary surgery, abortions or euthanasia. It requires them to abstain from sexual relations with patients, and to keep information divulged to them confidential. The oath was taken by doctors until 1948, when the World Medical Association created a modern restatement called the Declaration of Geneva

7 Catapult

Invented by Dionysios the Elder of Syracuse (c.430–367 BCE), the catapult can hurl heavy objects or shoot arrows over large distances. Having seized power in Sicily, Dionysios set about driving out the Carthaginians, who ruled a large part of the island. Thanks in part to the catapult, he was successful, making Syracuse the strongest power in Greek Italy.

The Romans later perfected his invention, adding wheels to catapults to make them mobile.

8 Greek Fire

Used as a secret weapon by the Byzantine Empire against enemy ships, Greek Fire was a highly flammable, jelly-like substance. It was blasted through bronze tubes mounted on the prows of Byzantine galleys, and was inextinguishable by water. It was first employed to repel an Arab fleet attacking Constantinople in 673, and then successfully used in combat until the late 12th century. Scientists are still unsure of its exact formula but think that it consisted of liquid petroleum, sulphur, naphtha and quicklime.

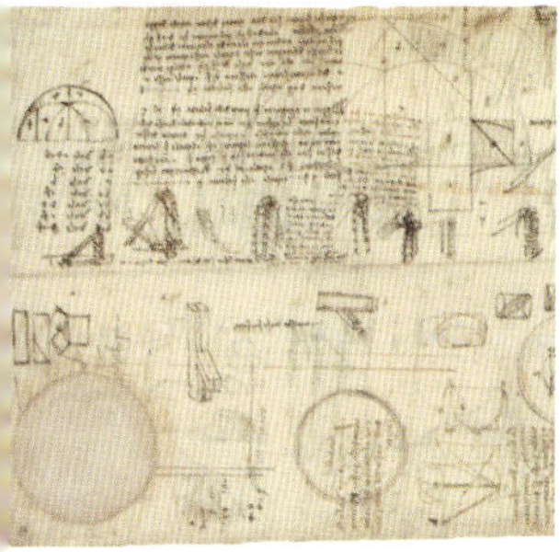

Leonardo da Vinci's sketch of Archimedes' Screw

9 Archimedes' Screw

The Syracusan-born Greek mathematician Archimedes (287–212 BCE) invented an ingenious water pump, which became known as Archimedes' screw. It consisted of a tube coiled around a rod, which is set at an angle, with the bottom end in water and a handle at the top. When the handle is rotated, the entire device turns and the tube collects water which is thus transported upwards.

10 Pap Smear

Since 1943, cervical cancer has been detected using the Pap smear test, a gynaecological procedure named after its inventor, the Athens-educated Greek-American doctor, George Papanikolaou (1883–1962).

TOP 10 OLYMPIC GAMES FACTS

1 The Olympic Truce
First adopted in 776 BCE when warring city states declared *ekecheira* (truce) to allow the Olympic games to take place during ancient times.

2 Decline of the Ancient Olympics
In 392–93 CE, the Christian Emperor Theodosios I banned all "pagan" observances, including the Olympics.

3 Revival of the Olympics
After 1,500 years the games were revived with the efforts of French Baron Pierre de Coubertin (1863–1937).

4 The First Modern Olympic Games
The first modern games were held in Athens, during April 1896 at the Kallimarmaro stadium.

5 The Olympic Rings
The five interlocking coloured rings represent the continents. It was designed by Baron de Coubertin in 1912.

6 The Olympic Medal
The last Olympic gold medals to be made entirely out of gold were awarded in 1912.

7 The Olympic Motto
The motto– *Citius, Altius, Fortius* (Swifter, Higher, Stronger) – was borrowed by Baron de Coubertin in 1921, from his late friend Henri Didon, a Dominican friar.

8 The Olympic Flame
In 1936, Carl Diem started the tradition whereby a torch ignited in Greece was transported by relay to the host city, and kept alight until the Games ended.

9 The First Olympic TV Broadcast
The 1936 Berlin Summer Olympic games were the first to be covered live on television.

10 The Second Modern Greek Games
In 2004, the Summer Olympics returned to Athens for the first time since 1896.

Lighting the torch in 2004, Athens

TOP 10 Artistic Styles

Angular Cycladic figurine

1 Cycladic, 3200–2000 BCE

The prehistoric Cycladic civilization flourished on the islands of Naxos, Paros, Amorgos, Milos, Syros and Keros (which form a rough circle around the holy island of Delos)) for over 1,000 years, before mysteriously disappearing. It left behind hundreds of marble figures: most are elegant, angular, minimalist female figures, probably used in a funerary or fertility cult.

2 Minoan, 2000–1400 BCE

The Minoans of Crete were sensual, social, nature-loving and matri-archal. Ceramics are painted with flowing lines based on natural motifs. Fluid-lined frescoes depict priestesses, bull-vaulting and animals. Most exciting are the faïence sculptures of voluptuous goddesses wielding snakes, and the fantastically light, delicate gold jewellery.

3 Mycenaean, 1600–1100 BCE

The art of this martial mainland culture was somewhat influenced by the Minoans. But they were fundamentally different, focused on war, order and acquisition, especially of gold. Their palaces housed hoards of embossed-gold swords, daggers, and cups, gold death-masks and pots painted with warrior images.

4 Geometric, 9th–7th Century BCE

Geometric art emerged from a dark age with vases painted with angular designs, and abstract, triangular-rectilinear human forms. The giant 8th-century BCE funerary vase in the National Archaeological Museum is iconic, where you can see the first "Greek key" pattern.

Admiring Archaic sculptures

5 Archaic, Mid-7th–Early 5th Century BCE

The start of monumental Greek art, with the first marble temples and sculptures. Early statues of young men and women, called *kouroi and korai respectively*, and made for religious purposes, were heavily influenced by Egyptian art: stiff, with carved and brightly painted garments and facial features.

6 Classical, 480–323 BCE

The advent of naturalistic sculptures balancing vibrancy and idealism. Temples were built according to mathematical proportions, adorned with tradition-shattering sculptural reliefs that seemed to break out from the marble. Many were created by the sculptor Pheidias, a central figure of Athens' Golden Age.

Reconstructed Mycenaean fresco

7 Hellenistic, 323 BCE–1st Century CE

Classical sculpture grew ripe and decadent, in part influenced by the new Hellenistic cities in the Orient, founded by Alexander the Great or his successors. The sculptor Lysippos defined the new phase with sensuous subjects such as Aphrodite, Pan and Dionysos in exaggerated, twisting movement.

14th-century Byzantine icon

8 Byzantine, c. 330–1500

Byzantine art was almost completely focused on depicting Christian images. Rich, colourful mosaics, frescoes, icons and religious objects were made with valuable materials, especially gold, and using intricate methods, which conveyed the wealth of the empire.

9 Ottoman Influence, 1453–1821

Under Islamic rule, monumental and public art was restricted, but folk arts flourished, incorporating aspects from the conqueror's culture, including intricate silver jewellery, metalwork, rugs, tapestries and embroideries.

10 Neo-Classical, 1836–Early 20th Century

The artistic tastes of independent Greece were determined by the Bavarian and Danish royal court and its architects, who were inspired by the Classical Greek monuments. Many of modern Athens' most important buildings were constructed on this model, notably the University of Athens, the Academy of Athens and the National Library.

TOP 10 ARTISTIC TERMS

1 Kouros/Kore
The first monumental sculptures in Greek art: a *kouros* was a youth, a *kore* a maiden. The plurals are *kouroi* and *korai* respectively.

2 Capital
The top of a column. There are three main Greek forms: Doric, a simple slab; Ionic, a carved scroll; and Corinthian, with an acanthus-leaf pattern.

3 Icon
Byzantine images of saints, believed to have holy power. They are often painted on a gold-leaf base.

4 Pediment
The triangular gable supported by columns on the temple's façade; often features relief sculptures.

5 Frieze
Horizontal band below the pediment of a temple, carved with decorative motifs.

6 Krater
A large ceramic or bronze bowl, often beautifully decorated, used for mixing wine and water.

7 Black-Figure Pottery
The earliest type of Greek vase painting, etched into red ceramic glaze, creating a somewhat stiff, formal image.

8 Red-Figure Pottery
A revolutionary method of Classical vase-painting. The outlines of figures are painted on with red glaze, creating flowing, active images.

9 Fresco
A painting made directly upon the plaster before it has dried, creating art that is integral to the wall.

10 Caryatids
Columns sculpted in the form of women. The most famous are at the Erechtheion at the Acropolis.

Caryatids at the Erechtheion

Following pages *Walkway at Athens' Olympic site*

TOP 10 City Strolls

Ermou, Athens' main shopping street

1 Ermou

This is Athens' most popular shopping street. Start at the top, with designer boutiques and department stores. Make your way down to the funkier end, where flea markets *(see p87)* are set up adjacent to the street. Beyond it are quirky used-furniture, antiques and speciality shops.

2 Dionysiou Areopagitou Walkway

A continuous pedestrian link between all the major archaeological sites in central Athens, this wide, tree-lined walkway has several open-air cafés.

3 Kallidromiou and Strefi Hill

Kallidromiou is the heart of Exárhia, especially on Saturdays, when the whole neighbourhood turns out for the open-air *laiki agora* (farmer's market). Soak up the sights of the street and buy some fresh fruit before heading to nearby Strefi Hill *(see p95)* for a healthy climb and bite to eat.

4 Philopappos Hill

Follow the winding paths to different monuments including two historic churches, a Roman memorial and Athens' old observatory. At the summit of this shady hill *(see pp34–5)*, enjoy extensive views over and beyond the city.

5 First National Cemetery of Athens

MAP D–E6

Take a contemplative walk through the wide, overgrown rows of handsome mausoleums in Athens' largest cemetery. It is thickly planted with cypress trees, whose tall, pointed shape the Greeks believe helps to guide souls up to heaven.

6 Lykavittos Hill

Several pleasant footpaths run through pine-clad Lykavittos Hill *(see p102)*. If you're feeling energetic, hike to the top; if climbing's not for you, take the funicular up and saunter down, stopping at the café for a drink.

Walking up Lykavittos Hill, overlooking the city

7 Zea (Pasalimani)

This natural harbour *(see p109)* at Piraeus is full of local fishing boats and yachts. Stroll around the marina, ending up on the west side, in front of the Nautical Museum, or come after dark when the many waterside cafés come to life.

8 Kallimarmaro Stadium

Ancient Panathenaic athletes and the runners of the first modern Olympics in 1896 ran laps in the sweltering centre of this beautiful marble stadium *(see p101)*. Modern joggers and walkers love the shady path on top of the 70,000-seat edifice. It is also used for concerts and rallies.

The landscaped National Gardens

9 National Gardens

The winding paths of the lush National Gardens *(see p101)* are a great place for a stroll. Started in 1839, this was a royal park, and the landscape was densely planted with 15,000 trees and flowers imported from around the world; many of those original plants still flourish.

10 Flisvos Marina

For a taste of cosmopolitan Athens, head to Flisvos Marina, where some of the most impressive yachts in the Mediterranean dock. A stroll along the promenade takes you past an outdoor shopping centre plus restaurants and cafés with sea views.

TOP 10 CITY VIEWS

Athens viewed from Areopagos rock

1 Areopagos
This high, slippery rock jutting over the Ancient Agora is where, for centuries, Athens' ruling council met.

2 Agios Georgios
The highest point in the city centre *(see p47)* offers views from the Parthenon all the way to the Saronic Gulf.

3 Philopappos Monument
Spectacular views directly across to the temples of the Acropolis or to Piraeus and the coast *(see p34)*.

4 Adrianou, Monastiraki
Sit in one of the many outdoor cafés lining this street *(see p80)* for a ring-side view of the ancient marketplace.

5 360 Cocktail Bar
A classic Monastiraki rooftop bar and café with prime views of the Acropolis.

6 GB Roof Garden
The magnificent views from the roof of the Grand Bretagne, a landmark itself, include the Parthenon, the parliament building and Mount Lykavittos.

7 Strefi Hill
In the shadow of Lykavittos, this green hill *(see p95)* is perfect if you desire a shorter climb but comparable views.

8 Athens Tower
Mesogeion 2
Greece's tallest building; no observation deck, but great views if you're visiting any of its companies.

9 Kesariani Monastery
Lovely monastery on the wooded slopes of Mount Hymettos, above Athens' eastern suburbs *(see p45)*.

10 Mount Pendeli
Up by the Astronomical Station in Athens' northernmost suburb, you get a great view of the city – day or night.

TOP 10 Off the Beaten Track

1 The Breeder Gallery

MAP B2 ■ Iasonos 45, Metaxourgio ■ Open noon–6pm Tue–Sat ■ www.thebreedersystem.com

West of Omonia, the up-and-coming (if somewhat seedy) neighbourhood of Metaxourgio is home to a growing number of art galleries, museums and trendy restaurants and cafés. Since 2008, the oldest and best-known gallery here, The Breeder, has showcased contemporary art. It promotes emerging Greek talent as well as exhibits works by established international artists.

2 Unexpected Athens Orientation Tour

MAP C2 ■ Meet at Platía Syntagma ■ Open 9:30am daily ■ Reservations essential ■ www.alternativeathens.com

Tour six historic neighbourhoods to uncover the story of how Athens began as a village and transformed into a sprawling city. You'll see an ancient river that still flows through the area and visit bustling markets.

Monastiraki, a stop on the Unexpected Athens Tour

3 Athens to the Coastline

■ Trekking Hellas, Parthenonos 12 ■ www.trekking.gr

See a different side of Athens on a four-hour cycle ride to the seaside, via appealing neighbourhoods. The tour is run by the enthusiastic and professional team at Trekking Hallas, who also offer sea kayaking at Cape Sounio, canyoning in the nearby Gorge of Goura, and an Artisans and Markets walk, among other options.

4 Athens Street Art

MAP C2 ■ Meet at Thissio Train Station ■ Open 10am daily ■ Reservations essential ■ www.alternativeathens.com

Athens is known for its graffiti artists, who make political statements with colour and humour on walls around the city. This three-hour tour takes you through Gazi, Metaxourgio and Psyrri, to reveal some of the city's most impressive graffiti.

5 Alibi Gallery

MAP B3 ■ Sarri 12, Psyrri ■ Open noon–2pm & 3–8pm Tue–Fri, noon–6pm Sat ■ www.alibigallery.com

Founded in 2013, this cutting-edge gallery features works by top local and international artists. They also encourage pop-up street-art events.

6 Cine Thision

MAP B5 ■ Apostolou Pavlou 7, Thisio ■ Open early May–late Oct, screenings 9pm & 11pm ■ Adm ■ www.cine-thisio.gr

Along Athens' loveliest pedestrian thoroughfare, between the Pnyx and the Areopagos, Athens' oldest *therino* (open-air summer cinema) dates from 1935. Locals flock here for outdoor films on balmy evenings. There's a bar for drinks and a magical view of the floodlit Acropolis. The vintage or recent films are in their original version, with Greek subtitles.

7 Culinary Secrets of Downtown Athens

MAP K3 ■ Meet at Platía Monastiraki ■ Open 9:30am Mon–Sat ■ Reservations recommended ■ www.culinarybackstreets.com

This walking-and-tasting tour lasts for five-and-a-half hours. It explores hidden eating joints in central Athens and regional dishes ranging from Macedonian-style *souvlaki* to Cretan recipes. Tastings are included in the fee.

8 Glyfada Beach

MAP T3 ■ Glyfada, 12 km (7.5 miles) from Athens, Attica coast ■ Open May–Oct ■ Adm

Few European capitals have beaches so close to the city centre. The tram from Syntagma takes you directly to Glyfada, a residential suburb with a sandy beach. In summer, locals arrive during their lunch break, take a dip, then go back to work. Stunning sunsets too.

9 Kesariani Monastery

A 25-minute bus ride from Syntagma, followed by a scenic 40-minute walk up the lower slopes of Mount Ymittos, brings you to this impressive 11th-century Orthodox monastery *(see p45)*, set amid unspoilt nature. The complex includes a Byzantine church with lovely 16th- and 17th-century frescoes, plus the ruins of the refectory, monks' cells and a bathhouse. Kesariani is occasionally visited by tour groups, but it mostly remains deserted.

Kesariani Monastery

10 Al Hammam

MAP K4 ■ Tripondon 16 ■ Open 1–9pm daily ■ www.alhammam.gr

Located in the heart of Plaka, and close to the historic Bath House of the Winds, this elegant marble Hamam offers a traditional Turkish bath experience, complete with an invigorating rubdown with a kese and olive soap bubble massage. All days at the Hammam baths are coed. It's a good idea to make a reservation in advance.

Glyfada Beach

Top 10 Greek Dishes

1 Moussakas

There are endless variations on this famous country casserole, but the basic ingredients – aubergine and minced lamb layered with potatoes and tomatoes, enriched with wine, spiced with nutmeg and topped with bechamel – stay the same. The flavour is warming and earthy.

2 Kouneli Stifado

This rich, tender wild rabbit stew comes from the mountains of northern Greece, where it still warms villagers every winter. The rabbit is spiced with tomatoes or vinegar, garlic and cinnamon, but its most wonderful characteristic is an unusual sweetness, achieved by the addition of dessert wine and lots of small onions, cooked until caramelized.

***Stifado*, or rabbit stew**

3 Horiatiki

A bastardized version appears on menus worldwide as "Greek salad". The real thing is just a matter of fresh ingredients. Sun-ripened tomatoes, crisp cucumbers, fiery red onions and green peppers, rich Kalamata olives, topped with a slab of feta, aromatic oregano or savoury vinegar, and extra-virgin olive oil make up this simple but soothing salad.

Horiatiki

Grilled octopus

4 Grilled Octopus

Best caught and served on the same day, having been grilled over hot coals, topped with oregano and drizzled with oil and vinegar. The texture should be tender and the taste salty-sweet.

5 Pites

Pites came to Greece from Turkey and the Middle East. The key to perfect *pites* (which means "pies") is the famous phyllo crust: dozens of layers of paper-thin, translucent dough, brushed with butter or olive oil and baked to light, flaky perfection. *Pites* can be sweet – like the honey, walnut and rosewater baklava – or savoury – like the *hortopita* made from wild greens or the spicy *kreatopita*, stuffed with minced meat.

6 Kokoretsi

This popular Greek rotisserie dish, served all year-round but especially during Easter, uses offal of a lamb or goat.Intestines are marinated in herbs, garlic and lemon juice, wrapped carefully around a spit and roasted for hours over coals, until it drips with flavourful juices.

7 Gemista

The name simply means "stuffed". Greeks pack tomatoes, aubergines, courgettes (zucchini), peppers and cabbage leaves with all manner of ingredients, including rice, herbs, raisins, pine nuts and an array of spices. The stuffed grape leaves are called *dolmadakia* or *yaprakia*.

8 Fasolada

The staple winter dish for the ancient Greeks, *fasolada* is still Greece's most popular soup. White beans, carrots, onions, celery and paprika are simmered in stock until tender, then topped with the crucial ingredient: extra-virgin olive oil. Olives and *toursi* (pickled vegetables) are traditionally served on the side.

Souvlaki **on a bed of vegetables**

9 Souvlaki

Souvla means a roasting spit, and this is the Greeks' favourite way to prepare meat. *Souvlaki* refers to the ubiquitous street favourite: bits of chicken, pork or lamb spit-roasted for hours. They are often basted with *tzatziki* (yogurt dip), and stuffed along with onions and tomatoes into a hot, freshly baked, oiled and fried pita bread.

10 Spetzofaï

Originating from Mount Pilion in Thessaly, this quick fry-up of sausages, aubergine, peppers and spices is a common dish and is found everywhere in Greece. There is a considerable amount of variation in this dish as each locale makes its own kind of sausages.

TOP 10 GREEK DRINKS

Aniseed-falvoured ouzo

1 Ouzo
Greece wouldn't be the same without ouzo. Drunk with *mezedes* (snacks), this aniseed-flavoured distillate can be up to 47 per cent alcohol.

2 Tsipouro
Similar to ouzo, this warm mainland drink is made from grape pomace left over from wine-making. Best for winters.

3 Retsina
The taste is not subtle, but affection for this wine with pine-resin-flavoured wine cuts across all age and class barriers.

4 Hyma (Bulk) Wine
Wine poured into tin measuring cups of glass flagons, preferably from barrels.

5 Dessert Wines
There are several noteworthy sweet fortified wines such as muscat-based white wine or the dark mavrodaphne.

6 Agiorgitikio Red Wines
"St George" grapes, usually from Nemea are the basis for some of the most popular, velvety Greek red wines.

7 Assyrtiko White Wines
Greece's star white grape – usually grown in Santorini but also found in Macedonia – is redolent of honey-suckle and figs.

8 Raki/Souma
Island favourites, raki and souma are other distillates made from either grape pomace or figs.

9 Greek Coffee
Powdered robusta beans are boiled in a long-handled *briki* (copper pot) and sweetened to taste.

10 Frappé
Instant coffee whipped into a delicious froth, ordered to desired sweetness, with or without milk.

TOP 10 Restaurants

1 Cookoovaya

This experimental restaurant *(see p107)* brings together five noted Greek chefs in a modern, open-plan kitchen. Try the *bourdetto*, a classic Corfiot fish dish, or *bianco*, fish served in a white sauce with potatoes.

Elegant dining at Cookoovaya

2 Point-a

Point-a is situated on the terrace of the Herodion Hotel *(see p146)*, and the restaurant's inventive, beautifully presented interpretations of Greek cuisine manage to hold their own against the competition of the astonishing view of the Acropolis.

3 Ergon House

Conceived as a contemporary agora, set inside a glass atrium, Ergon *(see p107)* is a fabulous destination in itself. An extensive menu of both traditional and modern Greek dishes is driven by excellence in ingredients: artisanal foods sourced from all over Greece, alongside the freshest produce from in-house urban gardeners, fishmongers, butchers and bakers.

4 Varoulko Seaside, Mikrolimano, Piraeus

Celebrity chef Lefteris Lazarou serves creative seafood dishes at waterside tables overlooking Mikrolimano *(see p112)*. Dishes such as grilled squid with black-eyed beans, marjoram and cumin, and oven-baked John Dory with cauliflower purée have earned him a Michelin star.

5 Mani Mani

Greek-American brothers add international style and a delicate, inspired touch to the cuisine here *(see p83)*. Menu highlights include pork tenderloin with soft cheese, figs, honey and almonds, or chickpeas with cumin, cabbage and fresh mint.

6 Nolan

At this chic restaurant *(see p90)* set in a minimalist space, chef Sotiris Kontizas draws on his multicultural upbringing by a Greek father and Japanese mother to create inspired seasonal comfort food, Greek-Asian style. Dishes like bean noodles with octopus and kalamata olives and gyoza with beef cheeks shine here.

7 Akra

At this dynamic addition to Athens' restaurant scene *(see p107)*, affordable fine dining becomes a reality. Top seasonal, local ingredients are interpreted with skill, while the bakery at the front of the restaurant offers fresh pastries. For a particularly sweet treat, order the caramelized milk tart for dessert.

Bakery and dining area of Akra

Two Michelin-starred Spondi

8 Spondi

The most sophisticated restaurant *(see p107)* in Athens has two Michelin stars and offers exquisitely prepared and presented haute cuisine by chef Angelos Lantos. Try dishes such as crab with turnip, honey, tarragon and passiflora, or venison in Sarawak pepper crust.

Hytra, Onassis Cultural Centre

9 Hytra

Michelin-starred chef Tassos Mantis serves spectacularly prepared and presented food *(see p83)*. There is an excellent eight-course degustation menu. Try the freshwater crayfish in basil and wild garlic sauce or the sea bass cooked with potato-leek cream and saffroned baby onions.

10 Orizontes

Perched on Lykavittos Hill, Orizontes *(see p107)* is an unforgettable dining venue. The city views are stunning, and the creative Mediterranean cuisine and extensive wine list are both excellent.

TOP 10 TAVERNAS

1 Klimataria
This historic taverna *(see p98)* is popular with locals due to its rembetika music, dancing and excellent dishes.

2 Nikitas
Excellent value *magirefta* (slow-cooked food) with decent bulk wine and friendly service *(see p90)*.

3 Filippou
Old-world taverna *(see p103)* in Athens' poshest neighbourhood. Specializes in Greek casseroles as well as grills and fish dishes.

4 Kapilio o Zachos
Try the crispy *gambari* (little shrimps) and homemade taramosalata at this neighbourhood favorite *(p112)*.

5 Ouzerie Lesvos
With the name of an island famed for ouzo, this charming place delivers the classic ouzo-meze experience.

6 To Kafenion
Delicious traditional food is served in cosy surroundings *(see p83)*.

7 Mouries
This traditional taverna *(see p107)*, serves excellent steam-trays. There are outdoor tables under mulberry trees.

8 Ama Lachei
Housed in an old-school house, this adorable taverna *(see p98)* has one of the most charming courtyards in town.

9 Thanassis
The house special here *(see p90)* is beef-based, spicy Egyptian style kebab.

10 Rififi
MAP D2 ▪ Emmanouil Benaki 69A & Valtetsiou ▪ 210 330 0237 ▪ €
A contemporary taverna with a summery pastel-hued decor. Lots for vegetarians, and good choice of beers and Greek distillates.

Relaxed and fun Rififi

TOP 10 Places to Shop

1 Parthenis

The relaxed lines and bohemian elegance of this definitive Greek fashion house *(see p105)* are synonymous with a cultured urban – and island – Greek lifestyle. Lines for men and for women are joined by unisex styles as well as sumptuous signature beach towels – a summer essential.

2 Benaki Museum Shop

MAP N3 ▪ Koumbari 1 & Vas. Sofias Ave

Find superb museum replicas, beautiful books and stylish contemporary homeware inspired by the permanent collection at the Benaki Museum's shop.

3 Melissinos Art

Come here *(see p89)* for made-to-measure handcrafted leather sandals, inspired by ancient Greek designs – perfect footwear for a summer on the beach. Melissinos' famous customers included The Beatles, Leonard Cohen and Kate Moss.

Athens' Flea Market

4 Loumidis Coffee Shop

The oldest surviving coffee roaster in Greece *(see p97)*. This place stocks a wealth of traditional Greek coffees, plus all the paraphernalia necessary for its preparation. It also sells a range of beans from around the world, as well as espresso machines, cups, shakers and all the accoutrements one could possibly desire for that perfect cup of coffee.

Entrance to Loumidis Coffee Shop

5 Athens' Flea Market

If you have an eye for antiques, you can pick up outstanding bargains at this sprawling and varied Sunday market *(see p87)*. Wake up early, though – there's not much point arriving here after 11am, as the streets become jam-packed and most of the treasures disappear quickly.

6 Giras Greek Arts and Crafts

MAP J3 ▪ Pandrossou 21, Plaka ▪ 210 322 1242

Old-school souvenir shops like this one were once the only option in Plaka, and they still serve a purpose; postcards, mementos and plenty of locally made, all-cotton clothing are well-priced at this nostalgic corner shop, run by the owner since 1974. A little piece of history and a fine place to stock up on gifts and souvenirs.

7 The Naxos Apothecary

MAP D4 ■ Kolokotroni 3-5, Voulis

Taking inspiration from Greece's oldest homeopathic pharmacy, the Naxos Apothecary specializes in natural medicines and remedies from the Cycladic Island of Naxos. The light and airy pharmacy stocks quality fragrances, superb creams, long-lasting candles and personalized herbal cosmetic remedies, all in beautiful, modern packaging, making the perfect gift or souvenir.

8 Zoumboulakis Gallery

MAP M3 ■ Kriezotou 6 ■ www.zoumboulakis.gr

A veritable Athenian institution, this shop showcases contemporary art, furniture, ceramics and sculptures. Also, there is an excellent range of limited-edition prints and posters by established artists, and exhibitions are held by up-and-coming Greek artists. Signed and numbered silkscreens are reasonably priced.

9 Kori

Bringing a new quality and sophistication to the words souvenir shop, Kori *(see p81)* stocks an eclectic mix of accessories and ornaments crafted by some of Greece's brightest and best young artists, as well as replicas of museum pieces and traditional pottery, icons and statuettes.

10 Pantopolion

A treasure trove for gourmands, this store *(see p81)* stocks an assortment of quality Greek regional produce, including thyme honey from Tinos, *mastiha* liqueur from Hios, black olives from Kalamata and dried herbs and teas from Mount Taygetos. Pantopolion is run by two retired lawyers, who also offer talks and organize tastings. They also package a selection of items in presentation boxes for you to take home.

Kori, a treasure trove of elegant Greek souvenirs

TOP 10 Athens for Free

Buskers on Platía Monastirakiou

1 Street Performers

Pass by Platía Monastirakiou *(see p86)* at almost any time of day to be entertained by street artists, who perform mime acts, fire-eating, juggling, busking and more.

2 Acropolis for Free

There is free entry to the Acropolis *(see pp12–13)* on 6 Mar (in memory of Melina Mercouri), 18 Apr (International Monuments Day), 18 May (International Museums Day), the last weekend of Sep (European Heritage Day), and 28 Oct (Ohi Day). The same applies to other key archaeological sites, including the Agora, Temple of Zeus and Hadrian's Library. Many sites and museums are also free on the first Sunday of the month during the winter.

3 The Benaki Museum of Greek Culture for Free

The Benaki Museum *(see pp26–7)* in Kolonaki traces the development of Greek culture through the ages and offers free entry every Thursday from 6pm, when it is also open until midnight.

4 Byzantine Break

On the busy shopping street of Ermou, peek inside tiny Kapnikarea *(see p87)*, a peaceful, 11th-century Byzantine church animated by flickering candles and bearded priests amid wafts of incense.

5 European Music Day

Each year on 21 June (the longest day of the year), free, open-air concerts take place throughout Greece, with the main stage in Athens on Platía Kotzia near Platía Omonia *(see p93)*.

6 Seaside Stroll

From Neo Faliro metro station, you can walk along the Akti Dilaveri to the coast to Piraeus, passing the fishing boats in the harbour at Mikrolimano *(see p111)*, flashy yachts moored up in Zea Marina *(see p109)* and informal cafés with fine sea views along Akti Themistokleous *(see p110)*.

Moored fishing boats and yachts in Piraeus

7 Tour the City with a Local

Enjoy an insider's experience of the city on a thematic walk with a resident Athenian *(see p139)*. In addition to exploring various neighbourhoods, tours also cover subjects such as architecture, LGBTQ+ Athens, street art and the flavors of the city. Tours are free, but tips are customary.

8 Performing Soldiers

The *evzones* – Greece's elite ceremonial guard – change hourly in front of the Tomb of the Unknown Soldier *(see p104)* at the Parliament Building. A larger ceremony takes place on Sundays at 11am.

Changing of the Guard ceremony

9 Panoramic Views

For a total escape from the urban bustle, hike up a steep winding path to the top of Lykavittos Hill *(see p102)* to enjoy glorious panoramic views over the entire city, with the sea and mountains visible in the distance. Great photo opportunities – and a free workout, too.

10 Market Colours

The Varvakios Central Market *(see p94)* offers a great Athenian shopping experience. You don't have to buy anything, but the stalls – piled high with seasonal fruit and vegetables, fresh seafood displayed on crushed ice and slightly gory meat products – make this a great venue for capturing local colour and atmosphere.

TOP 10 BUDGET TIPS

Travelling by ferry

1 Ferries going to the nearby islands, are slightly cheaper (although slower) than hydrofoils and catamarans.

2 When eating out, opt for *hyma* (bulk) wine, served by the carafe. It's cheap and cheerful, while bottled wine tends to be expensive.

3 In many bars, a table of meze with a carafe of raki costs the same as a couple of rounds of cocktails, so opt for that instead.

4 If you use public transport, be aware that a one-day travel ticket (valid for bus, tram and metro) costs €4.50; a five-day ticket €8.20. EU citizens over 65s, and under 18s, with ID cards receive a 50 per cent discount.

5 *Souvlaki* (kebab in pita bread) makes a tasty, nutritious takeaway meal, and is a cheap alternative to a sit-down lunch.

6 Many casual neighbourhood restaurants serve "*ladera*", an affordable and tasty dish, in which various vegetables are simmered in a tomato sauce.

7 Tap water in Athens is perfectly good to drink, so you don't have to buy bottled water. Bring a canteen instead.

8 Most of the main attractions in central Athens are within walking distance of one another, so you rarely need to use public transport. Just be sure to wear comfortable shoes.

9 The classic Athenian *kourou*, a shortcrust feta cheese pie, is a filing and inexpensive breakfast to start the day right.

10 At the beach, you have to pay for a sun bed or umbrella, so take a towel and straw mat and lie on the sand.

TOP 10 Festivals and Events

1 Epiphany
6 Jan

The "Blessing of the Waters", when young men dive for crosses cast into the water by priests at ports and beaches; it's a year's good luck for the successful divers.

2 Apokries
Feb–Mar

The Greek Orthodox Carnival begins 56 days before Easter Sunday. Festivities, especially glamorous masquerade parties, last for days. In Athens, the colourful celebrations centre on Plaka, where the streets are packed with revellers and masked musicians.

Flying kites on Clean Monday

3 Clean Monday
First day of Lent (Feb/Mar)

Greeks celebrate this day, which is also the Carnival's end by going to the country and flying kites; in Athens, the sky above Philopappos Hill is usually filled with them.

4 National Day/ Annunciation
25 Mar

Military parades with tanks, guns and battalions celebrate the start of the Greek independence revolt against the Ottomans in 1821. Annunciation to the Mother of God is also observed, linking religion and nationalism.

Eggs dyed red for Easter

5 Easter
Apr

This is the most important event on the Orthodox calendar, far outweighing Christmas. Highlights of the Holy Week include – Thursday evening Crucifixion liturgy; Friday processions by parishes parading flower-covered biers of Christ in effigy; the midnight Resurrection Mass on Saturday – concluding in fireworks (and, in remote villages, gunfire or tossed dynamite). On Sunday, families enjoy a meal of roast lamb, with eggs dyed red (symbolizing both the blood and rebirth of Christ).

6 Athens/Epidauros (Epidaurus) Festival
Jun–Aug ■ www.greekfestival.gr

Ancient Greeks performed timeless tragedies in the Odeon of Herodes Atticus, the Piraeos 260 and the theatres of Epidauros. Following this ancient tradition, every summer, the world's greatest singers, dancers and actors perform under moonlight at these venues. The festival has hosted Luciano Pavarotti, Martha Graham, Maria Callas and other luminaries.

Performance at the Epidauros festival

7 Athens Pride

May–Jun ■ www.athenspride.eu

Film screenings, talks, workshops, exhibitions, games and, of course, plenty of parties fill the warm spring days and nights, concluding with the Pride parade, a highlight.

8 Feast of the Dormition

15 Aug

Absolutely everything in town closes for the Dormition of the Mother of God, which is second only to Easter in the Orthodox calendar. Many "Marias" celebrate their name-day today (otherwise on 8 September or 21 November).

9 Athens Polytechnic Uprising

17 Nov

Parades commemorate the student revolt that happened at the National Technical University of Athens in 1973, which led to the end of the military dictatorship of 1967–1974.

Athens Marathon

10 Athens Marathon

Early/Mid-Nov

Athletes from around the world retrace the course of Pheidippides, antiquity's most celebrated runner. In 490 BCE, the Greeks defeated the Persians at Marathon in a historic battle for independence *(see p130)*. Pheidippides ran the 42 km (26 miles) to Athens, announced the outcome ("Victory!"), then died of exhaustion. Today's runners have the advantage of water stops, a cooler climate and cheering crowds en route from Marathonas to the Kallimarmaro Stadium *(see p101)* to ease the arduous feat.

TOP 10 SAINTS' DAYS

St Nicholas Day celebrations

1 Agios Vasilios/St Basil (1 Jan)
Families eat *Vasilopita* (Basil's cake), into which a coin has been baked. Finding the coin brings a year's good luck.

2 O Prodromos/St John the Baptist (7 Jan)
The day John baptised Christ in the Jordan river.

3 St Athanasios (18 Jan)
The church auctions off donated gifts in honour of Athanasios of Alexandria, one of Orthodoxy's three holy Fathers.

4 Agia Philothei (19 Feb)
Athens' patron saint, this 16th-century abbess was martyred for refusing to let Muslims seize her nuns for harem duties.

5 Agios Georgios/St George (23 Apr)
The dragon-slayer is the patron of the military and shephards.

6 Agia Irini/St Irene (5 May)
Born a 4th-century Persian princess, Irini became a zelous Christian. She is the patroness of the national police force.

7 Agios Dimitrios/St Demetrios (26 Oct)
Thessaloníki celebrates its patron saint and the city's reconquest by Greece in 1912.

8 St Catherine (25 Nov)
This famous Alexandrian martyr is honoured as the protectress of infants, maidens and female students.

9 St Stylianos (26 Nov)
Shown holding a swaddled infant, this is the patron of young children. He protects the unborn, and cures barrenness.

10 Agios Nikolaos/St Nicholas (6 Dec)
Celebrations honouring the patron saint of sailors are especially festive in coastal suburbs and on islands.

Athens Area by Area

Monastiraki Platía, with the Acropolis in the distance

TOP 10 Plaka, Makrygianni and Koukaki

The winding alleyways of Plaka, the old quarter below the Acropolis, are easily the most charming part of Athens. Naturally, they are also the most visited, and in midsummer some streets can be packed with touts and cheap gift stalls. But Plaka also conceals places of untouched delight. The formerly working-class areas of Makrygianni and Koukaki have shaken off old dust, and must-see museums, fine-dining restaurants and ultra-hip clubs are the new order of the day.

Relief sculpture on the Roman era, Tower of the Winds

PLAKA, MAKRYGIANNI AND KOUKAKI

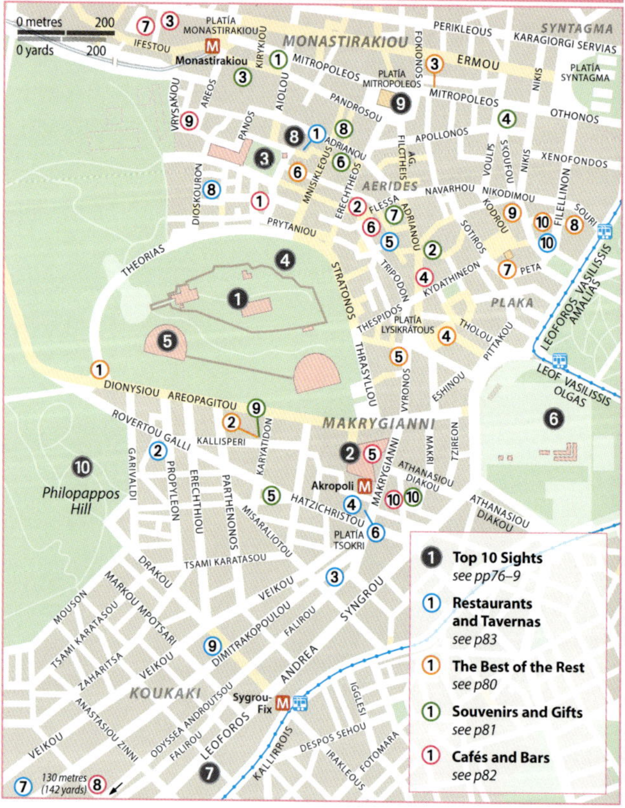

The impressive Acropolis, dominating the Plaka skyline

1 Acropolis

The sacred rock of the Acropolis *(see pp12–13)* dominates Plaka, and its different temples are clearly visible from all angles throughout the neighbourhood. Legend holds that it was on this rock that Athena *(see p53)* won dominion of Athens from Poseidon, and it has been devoted to worshipping the goddess since 650 BCE.

2 Acropolis Museum

Designed by internationally renowned architect Bernard Tschumi, this all-glass $100 million museum *(see p13)* opened in mid-2008. It was built to house the priceless Parthenon marbles *(see pp14–15)* in a modern, meaningful way, so that visitors could admire the historical works while looking out at the Acropolis, where the marbles were originally displayed.

Statue, Acropolis Museum

3 Roman Forum and Tower of the Winds

The Athenians, under Roman governor Nikias, built this Roman marketplace *(see pp24–5)*, which replaced the original Greek Agora, and the townspeople and Nikias are commemorated on the Gate of Athena Archegetis. Its most striking feature, the Tower of the Winds, was built around 50 BCE, during the rule of Julius Caesar. There was no other building like it in the ancient world: eight-sided, each side sculpted with a personification of the wind from that direction: Boreas, Kaikias, Apeliotes, Euros, Notos, Lips, Zephyros and Skiron.

4 Anafiotika

Clinging to the side of the Acropolis is Athens' loveliest and quirkiest neighbourhood. It was built during the 1830s by crafters from the Cycladic island of Anafi, brought to Athens after the War of Independence to build King Otto's palace. They re-created a pocket of home here, all island-style, blue-and-white houses, covered with banks of bougainvillea, in a maze of tiny passageways. Many descendants of the original Anafi workers still live here.

Peaceful courtyard in Anafiotika

LORD BYRON

Among Plaka's many famous residents was Romantic poet and philhellene Lord Byron (1788–1824), who lived in a monastery on Platía Lysikratous while writing *Childe Harold*. He fought on the Greek side in the War of Independence, and Athens remembers him in the street running south from Lysikratous: Vyronos (Byron in Greek).

Opera at the Odeon of Herodes Atticus

5 Odeon of Herodes Atticus

MAP B5 ■ Dionysiou Areopagitou ■ Closed for renovation until 2028 ■ www.aefestival.gr

Built at the base of the Acropolis, the Odeon of Herodes Atticus was endowed to Athens by the Athenian scholar and Roman consul who gave the theatre its name. The building still functions in its original role as a venue for musical performances – including opera, concerts and theatre – and its shows under the stars are a cultural highlight of the warmer months.

6 Temple of Olympian Zeus

All that remains of Greece's largest temple, a shrine to Zeus, is 16 columns. But, as they stand alone, silhouetted by the bright Attic sky, their majesty still overwhelms. Inside the temple was a colossal gold-and-ivory sculpture of the god, a copy of the original at Olympia, one of the Seven Wonders of the ancient world *(see pp36–7)*.

7 National Museum of Contemporary Art

MAP C6 ■ Kallirois & Frantzi, Makrygianni ■ 211 101 9000 ■ Adm ■ www.emst.gr

The long-awaited National Museum of Contemporary Art (EMST) opened in 2017 in the Fix building, a former brewery dating from 1957. Their permanent collection is small, but it is always worth calling in for the interesting temporary exhibits.

8 Museum of Greek Popular Musical Instruments

MAP K4 ■ Diogenous 1–3 ■ 210 315 0198 ■ Open 8:30am–3:30pm Wed–Mon ■ Adm

Located in the historic Lassanis Mansion, one of the oldest surviving buildings of Plaka, this intimate museum is the work of musicologist Foivos Anogoianakis. Here visitors gain an appreciation for traditional Greek music and its influences as well as traditional instruments such as the bouzouki, mandoline, lyra and santouri, which are themselves works of art.

Temple of Olympian Zeus

Entrance to Mitropoli

9 Mitropoli

MAP K3 ■ Platía Mitropoleos ■ Open 6:30am–8pm daily

The lavish Athens Metropolitan Cathedral *(see p47)* is one of the city's best-known landmarks. The archbishop of Greece gives addresses here, and it is regularly packed for Athens' high-society weddings. Of greater artistic importance, though, is tiny Panagia Gorgoepikoös ("little Mitropoli"), next door. This 12th- century church incorporates Hellenistic, Roman and Byzantine masonry, depicting ancient feasts.

Monument at Philopappos Hill

10 Philopappos Hill

Next to the Acropolis rock, pine-and-cypress-clad Philopappos Hill *(see pp34–5)* offers a cool, green place to stroll. The peak, marked by the tomb and monument of Roman-Syrian prince Gaius Julius Antiochos Philopappos, offers sweeping views from the Acropolis to the sea. In summer, the Dora Stratou Dance Troupe puts on regular performances of Greek folk dances in a theatre nestled among the pines.

A MORNING IN PLAKA

EARLY MORNING

Hike up to the **Acropolis** *(see p77)* early, to beat the heat and the worst of the crowds. Spend an hour or so admiring the temples.

Come down from the Acropolis and turn left onto the **Dionysiou Areopagitou** walkway *(see p60)*. Your Acropolis ticket gives you free entry into the **Theatre of Dionysos** *(see p13)*, where many great classical dramas were first staged.

Head back out to the walkway to visit the **Acropolis Museum** *(see p77)*. Next, head to **Platía Lysikratous**, named after the unusual monument to the winner of a 335 BCE choral competition. Stop for a frappé in one of the leafy cafés nearby.

LATE MORNING

From the square, head up to the charming 19th-century quarter of **Anafiotika** *(see p77)* to explore its twisting alleys.

Leave by Prytaniou, stopping in the quiet garden of the Byzantine **Church of the Holy Sepulchre** *(see p80)*, and lighting a candle from its famed holy flame.

From Prytaniou, turn right on Mnisikleous and left on Kyrristou for a choice of either the **Museum of Greek Musical Instruments**, while it is still at this location, or the **Roman Forum and Tower of the Winds** *(see p77)*. Finally, head back a block to **O Platanos** *(see p83)*, for a hefty Greek lunch under a huge plane tree.

See map on p76

The Best of the Rest

1 Pikionis Pathway

MAP J5

In the 1950s, Greek architect Dimitris Pikionis and his team used reclaimed marble to create a path around the Acropolis, starting at the base and snaking all the way to the top.

2 Lalaounis Museum

MAP J5 ■ Kallisperi 12 & Karyatidon ■ 210 922 1044 ■ Open 9am–3pm Mon–Sat ■ Adm

Jeweller Ilias Lalaounis showcases his creations at this museum.

Jewellery at Lalaounis Museum

3 Maria Callas Museum

MAP C4 ■ Mitropoleos 44 ■ Apr–Oct: 10am–7pm Tue–Sun (to 9pm Fri); Nov–Mar: 10am–6pm Tue–Sun (to 8pm Fri) ■ Adm ■ www.mariacallasmuseum.gr

Greek-American soprano singer La Divina is celebrated at this museum through immersive exhibits and displays of personal artifacts.

4 Church of Agia Ekaterini

MAP L5 ■ Off Platia Lysikratous

The columns of an ancient temple still stand beneath the courtyard of this lovely Byzantine church.

5 Choregic Monument of Lysikrates

MAP L5 ■ Platia Lysikratous

This monument, honouring a Dionysian choral competition sponsor, is a favourite Plaka landmark.

6 The Bath House of the Winds

MAP K4 ■ Kyrristou 8 ■ 210 324 5957 ■ Open 8am–3:30pm Wed–Mon ■ Adm

A refurbished Ottoman bath-house from the 16th century, this small museum places public baths in their social context.

7 Frissiras Museum of Contemporary European Painting

MAP L4 ■ Monis Asteriou 3 & 7 ■ 210 323 4678 ■ Open 11am–6pm daily (to 5pm Sat & Sun) ■ Adm ■ www.frissirasmuseum.gr

A museum of over 3,000 works of top post-war Greek and European artists.

8 Agia Triada

MAP L4 ■ Filellinon

The largest medieval church in the city dates originally from 1031 and is now Athens' Russian Orthodox church.

9 Museum of Greek Children's Art

MAP L4 ■ Kodrou 9 ■ 210 331 2621 ■ Open 10am–2pm Tue–Fri ■ Closed Aug ■ Adm

Admire works by young artists living in mountain tribes, cities and refugee centres. Many activities for kids.

10 Jewish Museum

MAP L4 ■ Nikis 39 ■ 210 322 5582 ■ Open 9am–4pm Mon–Fri, 10am–4pm Sun ■ Adm ■ www.jewishmuseum.gr

The collection's 15,000 items tell the story of the Jews in Greece.

Exhibit at the Jewish Museum

Souvenirs and Gifts

Arts and crafts objects for sale at Forget Me Not

1 Pantopolion

MAP M3 ■ Dimitrakopoulou 34

This is the place *(see p69)* to purchase traditional Greek foodstuffs made by monks at Makariotissa Monastery in Viotia, plus a vast selection of Greek wines and local craft beers.

2 Ioanna Kourbela

MAP C4 ■ Adrianou 109 ■ ionnakourela.com

Youthful, flowing clothes made from natural organic fabrics such as cotton, linen, wool and silk.

3 Pagani

MAP C4 ■ Pandrosou 59 ■ www.pagani.gr

This handmade decorative arts shop features crafts and jewellery reflecting Greek tradition and culture.

4 Kori

MAP K3 ■ Mitropoleos 13 & Voulis ■ www.kori.gr

This little shop sells signed and numbered artworks by some of the country's latest talents.

5 Little Tree Books and Coffee

MAP C6 ■ Kavalotti 2 ■ 210 924 3762

A great spot for a coffee break near the Acropolis Museum *(see p13)*, with a selection of books in English, plus sketchbooks on sale.

6 Forget Me Not

MAP C4 ■ Adrianou 100 ■ www.forgetmenotathens.gr

This gift shop offers unusual items by contemporary Greek designers, including T-shirts, ceramics and jewellery.

7 Flaneur

MAP K4 ■ Adrianou 110

There's no city more suited to a long stroll than Athens – stock up here on chic and sustainable supplies for your foot-powered adventure, plus stylish necessities from Greek designers.

8 Olive Tree Store

MAP C4 ■ Adrianou 67

This family-run store stocks bowls, spoons and chopping boards made from olive wood. They also arrange shipping.

9 Lalaounis Museum Jewellery Shop

MAP J5 ■ Corner of Karyatidon & Kallisperi 12

Some of the world's most glamorous gold creations are to be found at Ilias Lalounis' celebrated jewellery house.

10 True Story

MAP K6 ■ Makriyianni 33 ■ www.true-story.gr

Exquisite items from Greek designers include affordable jewelry, scarves and clever housewares.

See map on p76

Cafés and Bars

1 Klepsydra
MAP K4 ■ Klepsydra

This tiny, quiet bar-café located beyond the Tower of the Winds is surrounded by flower pots and pastel-hued buildings.

2 Melina
MAP K4 ■ Lysiou 22, Aerides

This pink-and-gilt shrine to the late Greek actress and national heroine Melina Mercouri was once her favourite café.

3 Couleur Locale
MAP J3 ■ Normanou 3

This rooftop bar serves excellent coffee and other drinks, and offers one of the most stunning views of the Acropolis in Plaka.

4 O Brettos
MAP L4 ■ Kydathineon 41

The walls here are lined with bottles of home-made, brilliantly coloured liquors that glow like stained-glass windows. The drinks are good, too.

5 Acropolis Museum Café
MAP C5 ■ Dionysiou Areopagitou 15

Located on the museum's ground floor, this café-restaurant serves coffee, drinks and light snacks on a terrace overlooking the excavations found under the museum. There is free admission at the ticket desk for those coming just for the café.

6 Cafe Plaka
MAP C5 ■ Tripodon 1

Set on a quaint rooftop terrace in the heart of Plaka on Tripodon, this spot serves coffee along with sweet and savory snacks.

7 TAF-The Art Foundation
MAP B4 ■ Normanou 5

This multi-purpose art and culture space is housed in a beautiful 19th-century building, and has a convivial bar-café located in the inner courtyard. It can be hard to find: look for the small wooden door.

8 Koukles
MAP C6 ■ Zan Moreas 32 ■ 694 755 7443

The drag show at this Koukaki club gets rave reviews, as does the friendly service.

9 Vryssaki
MAP J3 ■ Vrysakiou 17, Plaka

An arts venue and bar, with rooftop terrace overlooking the Ancient Agora, Vryssaki encourages all sorts of experimental activities.

10 Hitchcocktales
MAP K6 ■ Porinou 10, Makrygianni

Set in a refurbished industrial space, this place is open only at night. It serves food and drinks with menu names inspired by Alfred Hitchcock's films.

Interior of the Acropolis Museum Café

Restaurants and Tavernas

1 O Platanos

MAP K4 ■ Diogenous 4 ■ 210 322 0666 ■ Closed Sun ■ No credit cards ■ €

Eat grilled or oven-baked meat accompanied by *horta* (amranth greens), washed down with some of the best *retsina (see p65)* in Attica.

The historic Strofi restaurant

2 Strofi

MAP B5 ■ Rovertou Galli 25 ■ 210 921 4130 ■ €€

Offers great rooftop views and food that is a cut above the typical taverna fare. Audience and performers from the Herodes Atticus often come here.

3 Mani Mani

MAP C6 ■ Falirou 10 ■ 210 921 8180 ■ €€

At this stylish restaurant, a spiral staircase leads to modern dining rooms with just a hint of rustic style. On the menu is nouvelle mainland cuisine.

4 Namaste

MAP K6 ■ Lempesi 12 ■ 210 923 3999 ■ Closed Mon ■ €

Tuck into superb curries, tandoor specialities, freshly baked naan and a great array of vegetarian options.

PRICE CATEGORIES

For a three-course meal for one with half a bottle of wine (or equivalent meal), taxes and extra charges.

€ under €40 **€€** €40–€60 **€€€** over €60

5 To Kafenion

MAP K4 ■ Epiharmou 1 & Tripodon ■ 210 324 6916 ■ €

Located on a side street, this is often missed by tourists. Regional dishes are lifted with home-made sauces.

6 To Kati Allo

MAP K6 ■ Hatzichristou 12 ■ 210 922 3071 ■ €

On the street flanking the Acropolis Museum to the south, this small family-run tavern offers delicious Greek comfort food.

7 Garyfallo Kanela

MAP B6 ■ Odyssea Androutsou 35, Koukaki ■ 210 924 5332 ■ Closed Sun D ■ €

Homestyle, aromatic casserole dishes with options for vegetarians. They serve three kinds of *hyma* wine *(see p65)*.

8 Dioskouroi

MAP J4 ■ Dioskouron 13, Plaka ■ 210 321 9607 ■ €

At the tourist heart of Athens, this café-taverna draws locals and visitors alike with its impressive ringside view of the Ancient Agora.

9 Kalamaki Bar

MAP C6 ■ Drakou 15 ■ 21 1017 1862 ■ €

This welcoming grill house on a tree-shaded street has well-priced fare, which can be enjoyed with house wine by the glass or a carafe.

10 Iliada

MAP D5 ■ Kidathineon 1–3 ■ 211 407 6438 ■ €

A popular gyros spot that serves homemade classics such as falafel and pita with beer available on tap.

See map on p76

TOP 10 Monastiraki, Psyrri, Gazi and Thisio

For decades, these old neighbourhoods of warehouses and workshops lay quiet, crumbling and neglected, enlivened only by the Monastiraki flea market, which spills out antiques, books and charming memorabilia from Platía Avissynias, and is popular with locals and visitors alike. This part of the city is a hub for alternative clubs, cafés and restaurants. Gentrification hasn't robbed these districts of their character, though. Rather, craft shops and industrial buildings nestle side-by-side with trendy clubs, hole-in-the-wall Greek music dives and squares filled with outdoor cafés and bars. Adding to the mix are a staggering number of marble antiquities at the Ancient Agora and Kerameikos, Athens' greenest archaeological sites.

An exhibit at Technopolis

1 National Observatory of Athens

MAP A5 ■ Hill of the Nyphs ■ Opening hours vary, check website ■ 210 349 0160 ■ www.noa.gr

The beautiful hilltop Neo-Classical observatory, a sight in itself, hosts tours and observations through the historical Doridis telescope.

2 Hadrian's Library

MAP J3 ■ Opening hours vary, check website ■ Adm ■ www.odysseus.culture.gr

Roman Emperor Hadrian built this sumptuous "library" (really more of

Ruins of Hadrian's Library

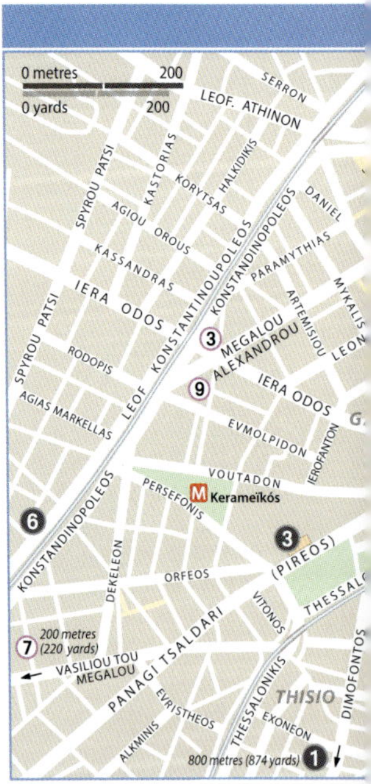

a luxurious forum) in 132 CE *(see p44)*. It featured a marble courtyard, mosaic floors, concert areas and a small area for storing library scrolls, all surrounded by exquisite Corinthian columns.

3 Technopolis

MAP A4 ■ Pireos 100 ■ www.athens-technopolis.gr

Dating from 1862, this enormous complex is housed in a former gasworks which functioned until 1984, giving the area its name (Gazi). In 1999 it was converted into a huge arts centre, hosting top-notch exhibitions, concerts and arts spaces. The creation of Technopolis revitalized the entire area, making Gazi one of the liveliest nightlife hubs of the city.

4 Kerameikos

A green oasis in the middle of factories and transportation depots, this is the site of the oldest and largest burial ground in Attica

Kerameikos burial ground

(see pp30–31). There are walls and gates of the ancient city, and running through the latter is the Sacred Way. Outside the site, the road continues – still incongruously named Sacred Way despite its congested traffic and often empty warehouses.

MONASTIRAKI, PSYRRI, GAZI AND THISIO

5 Platía Monastirakiou

MAP J3

There has been a church and monastery on this site since at least the 10th century. After most of the monastic buildings were lost during 19th-century excavations, the area was renamed Monastiraki – "little monastery". Built in 1678, the Pantánassa church, is dedicated to the Dormition of the Mother of God.

Platía Monastirakiou

6 Benaki Pireos Annexe

MAP A4 ■ Pireos 138 ■ Adm ■ www.benaki.org

In a renovated 1960s Lada car showroom, this modern exhibition space stages temporary art shows, with an emphasis on contemporary photography, painting, sculpture, installations and architecture. Similar to the main Benaki Museum of Greek Culture, there's a gift shop and small bistro-café. The building envelopes a central courtyard, which is used for open-air summer performances.

THE JEWISH COMMUNITY

The area of Psyrri and Kerameikos has been heavily settled by Greek Jews since the 3rd century BCE. In 1944, the Nazis occupying Athens sent more than half the population to concentration camps; however, the community has slowly recovered to about 3000, and has become a centre of Greek Jewish life.

7 Platía Agias Irinis

MAP K3 ■ Aiolou St & Skouze

This popular square has lived many lives, from being a 19th-century business district to a flower market and even a garment district. Neglected for a few decades, it regained its splendour and found a new identity during the 2000s, owing to Aiolou's pedestrianisation, as a hotspot for trendy yet traditional restaurants, stylish bars and cafés located around the butter-coloured Agia Irini church, dating from 1850s.

8 Agora and Agora Museum

One of the most interesting archaeological sites in Greece, the Agora *(see pp16–19)* is where Socrates "corrupted" youth, St Paul preached and converted his first followers, and the first decisions in the fledgling Athenian democracy were made. Don't miss the wonderfully preserved Temple of Hephaistos, or the recreated Stoa of Attalos, now home to the excellent Agora Museum.

Covered walkway of the Stoa of Attalos, which houses the Agora Museum

9 Kapnikarea

MAP K3 ■ Kapnikarea & Ermou ■ Open 8am–2pm daily

One of Athens' greatest pleasures is walking down a crowded street and suddenly finding yourself face-to-face with a tiny, centuries-old monument in the midst of all the modernity. The beautiful 11th-century church known as Kapnikarea, smack in the middle of the shopping street of Ermou and beautifully decorated with frescoes by master Photis Kontoglou in the 1950s, provides just such a moment. Possibly built over the ruins of an ancient shrine to a goddess, the church is appropriately dedicated to the Presentation of the Mother of God.

Photis Kontoglou frescoes, Kapnikarea

10 Athens' Flea Market

MAP J3 ■ Platía Avissynias & Ifestou

Platía Avissynias comes alive on Sunday mornings, when Athens' biggest and most colourful flea market fills the space and spills out to the streets around it. Here's where you'll find a little bit of everything: pink cut-glass Turkish liqueur sets, old and ornate phones that still work, beautiful antique carved-wood desks, and piles of fantastic kitsch curiosities. Use your haggling skills. Shops in Ifestou, which is close by, are open daily.

SUNDAY MARKETS

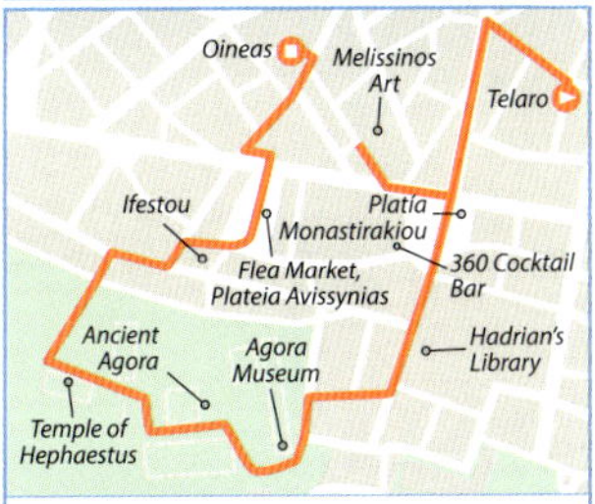

MORNING

Start the day at **Telaro** *(Aiolou 33; 210 32 43 840)* diagonally opposite Agia Irini church and marvel at the chanting after 9:30am.

Next, head for Psyrri to **Melissinos Art** *(see p89)*. The third generation owner continues to create custom fit sandals at this family shop that has been in business since 1920.

Proceed to the historic church at the centre of **Platía Monastirakiou**, and then take a coffee break at **360 Cocktail Bar** *(see p61)* and enjoy the lovely Acropolis views. Next, stroll towards the ancient halls and courtyard of **Hadrian's Library** *(see pp84–5)*.

EARLY AFTERNOON

Head over to the **Ancient Agora**, the sprawling marketplace that was Athens' heart for centuries. Make sure not to miss the wonderfully well-preserved **Temple of Hephaistos** *(see p16)* and the restored Stoa of Attalos, home to the excellent **Agora Museum**.

Cross over the metro tracks to **Ifestou** for the fun of haggling at the lively **Athens' Flea Market** at Platía Avissynias. It's hard to resist buying at least something, though by this stage of the day it is more likely to be an unusual collection of bric-a-brac than charming antiques at bargain prices.

Once you're done, retire with your booty to **Oineas** *(p90)* to enjoy a long lunch, while the marketplace closes down and the music and drinking start up.

See map on pp84–5

The Best of the Rest

Flea market in front of Tzisdarakis Mosque

1 Tzisdarakis Mosque

MAP C4

With a brightly painted mihrab, this 18th-century mosque houses specialist ceramics. It is believed that the building incorporates a pillar from the Temple of Olympian Zeus.

2 Thiseon Open Air Cinema

MAP B5 ■ Apostolou Pavlou 7 ■ www.cine-thisio.gr

A film under the stars is a memorable Greek summer pleasure. You can find few better settings than Cine Thiseon, with its fine Parthenon views.

3 Bernier/Eliades Gallery

MAP A4 ■ Eptahalkou 11 ■ www.bernier-eliades.gr

This premiere gallery exhibits local as well as international artists.

4 Hammam Bathing House Athens

MAP B3 ■ Melidoni 1, Agion Asomaton ■ www.hammam.gr/en/athens

For a traditional Turkish bath experience, visit the Hammam right next to the Benaki Museum of Islamic Art.

5 Beth Shalom Synagogue

MAP B4 ■ Melidoni 3

Originally Sephardic, this is Athens' main synagogue. Before World War II, this area was the centre of the city's Jewish community. There is an older and smaller synagogue at Melidoni 8.

6 The Project Gallery

MAP J3 ■ Normanou 3 ■ www.theprojectgallery.gr

Besides international exhibitions of contemporary art, this gallery also hosts talks and live performances.

7 Adrianou

MAP K3

This lively street runs along the edge of the Ancient Agora with the Acropolis in the background.

8 Herakleidon Museum

MAP A4 ■ Iraklidon 16 & Apostolou Pavlou 37 ■ Open Apr–Oct: 10am–6pm daily; Nov–Mar: 10am–6pm Wed–Sun ■ www.herakleidon-gr.org

Offering exceptional gift items, this private museum also has permanent as well as temporary exhibits.

Exhibition at Herakleidon Museum

9 Benaki Museum of Islamic Art

MAP B3 ■ Agion Asomaton 22 & Dipylou ■ www.benaki.gr

Set inside a Neo-Classical town house, this museum has four large exhibition rooms displaying Islamic ceramics, woodcarvings, metalwork, glassware and textiles.

10 Odos Iraklidon

MAP A4

Lined with cafés and bars, this crowded street feels both old world and fresh, and bustles day and night.

Markets and Antiques

1 Bahar

MAP K2 ■ Evripidou 31–33

The whole area around the central meat market teems with old, family-run shops selling traditional foodstuffs. Bahar is one of the best-known for herbs and spices.

2 Artemis

MAP K2 ■ Aristidou 6

You never know what you might unearth among the books, coins, stamps, jewellery and antiques in this potential treasure trove.

3 Athens' Flea Market

Everything under the sun, from ancient coins to fake designer sunglasses, frilly knickers and genuine antiques at rock-bottom prices *(see p87)*.

4 D. Gounaris

MAP J3 ■ Ifaistou 11

A tiny alcove manages to stock a fine selection of traditional wooden *tavli* (backgammon) boards as well as chess sets. Prices from as low as €10.

5 3Quarters

MAP C3 ■ Agiou Dimitriou 19 ■ 211 183 2311

In Psyrri, this store sells street-chic, user-friendly bags and backpacks. All its products are made from a sustainable source – locally acquired, unused and unwanted awning fabric.

Antiques at Martinos

7 Martinos Antiques

MAP K3 ■ Pandrosou 50 ■ www.martinosart.gr

Three-floor shop offering furniture, gold and silver, paintings, carpets and books from all over the world.

8 Vasilis Korovessis

MAP J3 ■ Adrianou 7 ■ 210 321 7562

A charming shop packed with books, engravings, exquisite old maps, photographs and postcards.

6 Melissinos Art

MAP L4 ■ Tzireon 16 ■ www.melissinos-art.com

"Poet sandal-maker" Stavros Melissinos took over his father's shop for handmade leather sandals in 1954, which has drawn a lot of celebrity clientele. The shop is still a favourite, with over 30 basic styles of sandals.

Sandals from Melissinos Art

9 Hyper-Hypo

MAP C4 ■ Voreou 10 ■ www.hyperhypo.gr

At Hyper-Hypo, you'll find an array of books and magazines on contemporary Greek art, design and culture.

10 Kalyviotis

MAP L3 ■ Ermou 8

Thread and fabric, bead- and button-filled shops populate the area around Ermou and Perikleous. Kalyviotis is the best one-stop haberdashery.

See map on pp84–5 ←

Places to Eat

PRICE CATEGORIES
For a three-course meal for one with half a bottle of wine (or equivalent meal), taxes and extra charges.

€ under €40 €€ €40–€60 €€€ over €60

1 Nolan

MAP L3 ■ Voulis 31, Athina 105 57 ■ 210 324 3545 ■ €

Recent Masterchef judge and popular chef Sotiris Kontizas creates inspired comfort food, Greek-Asian style.

Traditional interior of Oineas

2 Oineas

MAP J2 ■ Esopou 9, Psyrri ■ 210 321 5614 ■ €

High-quality, modern taverna food with a twist. Share a massive house salad, then try the stuffed lamb, or the orzo hotpot with crayfish.

3 Thanassis

MAP K3 ■ Mitropoleos 69 ■ 210 324 4705 ■ €

Athens' most famous *souvlaki* and beef kebab joint has been serving up sliced meat, with cool *tzatziki*, wrapped in pittas, since the 19th century.

4 Aiolou 68

MAP K2 ■ Aiolou 68 ■ 210 324 7925 ■ €

Fresh fish and seafood classics in a delightful contemporary space near the central fish market.

A plate of *souvlaki*

5 Veganistan

MAP A3 ■ Keramikou 101, near Plateon ■ 213 099 5581 ■ €

This collective serves a variety of vegan fusion street food dishes made from organic ingredients in a casual storefront setting with outdoor seating.

6 Ta Karamanlidika Tou Fani

MAP J2 ■ Evripidou 52 at Sokratous, Psyrri ■ 210 325 4184 ■ €

With in a renovated Neo-Classical interior, this deli-*mezedopolio* serves inner-Anatolian (Karamanian) influenced recipes such as pickled okra and 'finger' kebab in yogurt sauce.

7 Aleria

MAP A3 ■ Megalou Alexandrou 57, Metaxourgio ■ 210 522 2633 ■ €€€

Come here for crab with fennel and kohlrabi, sweetbreads with fricassee, or a choice of tasting menus.

8 Shedia

MAP K3 ■ Kolokotroni 56 ■ 210 331 6849 ■ €

Set up to create job opportunities for those who have experienced extreme poverty. Shedia offers a menu of delicious organic dishes designed by Michelin-starred chef Lefteris Lazarou, who also trained the cooks.

9 Hill

MAP B4 ■ Apostolou Pavlou 27 ■ 210 346 9077 ■ €€

This restaurant serves elegant, creative Greek cuisine, and has sweeping views of the Parthenon.

10 Nikitas

MAP J2 ■ Agion Anargyron 19, Psyrri ■ 210 325 2591 ■ €

Founded in 1967, this is probably the oldest taverna in Psyrri. The menu includes delicious grills and an excellent beer and wine selection.

Nightspots

Live music at Six D.O.G.S

1 MoMix
MAP J2 ■ Agioi Anargiron 21 ■ www.momixbar.com

Sample unique cocktails based on molecular mixology at this creative music bar. Conventional drinks and light meals are available, too.

2 BEqueer
MAP A4 ■ Keleou 10

Great dance music and entertaining drag shows, plus a welcoming and safe atmosphere, make this a Gazi favourite.

3 Noel
MAP K2 ■ Kolokotroni 59B, Monastiraki

Set in the historic Kourtaki arcade, this bistro-bar has a quirky decor. It is famous for its fine cocktail menu.

4 Baba au Rum
MAP C4 ■ Klitiou 6

Sip local cocktails prepared with premium spirits, fresh juices and homemade syrups and liqueurs.

5 Romantso
MAP C3 ■ Anaxagora 3 ■ 216 700 3325

Gorgeous industrial space with mid-century furnishings, perfect for culture, concerts, coffee and cocktails.

6 A for Athens
MAP J3 ■ Miaouli 2–4

This sleekly designed rooftop bar offers views of Plaka and the Acropolis. Come for breakfast or an evening cocktail.

7 Beaver Cooperativa
MAP A4 ■ Megalou Vasileiou 46A

This welcoming and inclusive women's cooperative has a great LGBTQ+ bar and a menu of delicious vegan and vegetarian selections. It is pet friendly.

8 Bios
MAP B3 ■ Pireos 84, Gazi

The street level bar is another of Athens' most impressive industrial spaces, with vintage airline signage. Bios also stages alternative theatre and concerts. The rooftop bar has great views of the Acropolis.

9 Sodade2
MAP A3 ■ Triptolemou 10 ■ 210 346 8657

This well-established gay bar and dance club in Gazi is known for an excellent music selection – house, Greek pop, classic hits. The staff here is friendly and the overall mood great.

Trendy Booze Cooperativa

10 Booze Cooperativa
MAP C4 ■ Kolokotroni 57

An arty club with exhibitions, videos and alternative theatre. Downstairs are magazines and board games; upstairs is loud rock music.

See map on pp84–5 ←

TOP 10 Omonia and Exárhia

Black-figure wine jug with a libation scene

Embodying Athens at its most urban, Exárhia and Omonia are among the city's oldest, most well-worn districts. Both have borne witness to a complex history: in 1973, the Polytechnic student uprising in Exárhia was crushed by the junta, but it did eventually lead to the fall of the military dictatorship. Today, Exárhia is a haven of intellectual conversation, street art and great cafés and bars; it is also the best place to hear rembetika, the Greek blues. Below Exárhia is clamorous Omonia, and just beyond is the robust marketplace district.

1 Municipal Art Gallery

MAP B3 ■ Myllerou 32 & Leonidou ■ Open 11am–7pm Tue–Sat, 10am–3pm Sun

All of the best-known modern Greek artists are represented here, in addition to works by 19th-century Saxon architect Ernst Ziller. On display are his plans for the Neo-Classical National Theatre and for the city's grandest private homes, now mostly converted to museums.

OMONIA AND EXÁRHIA

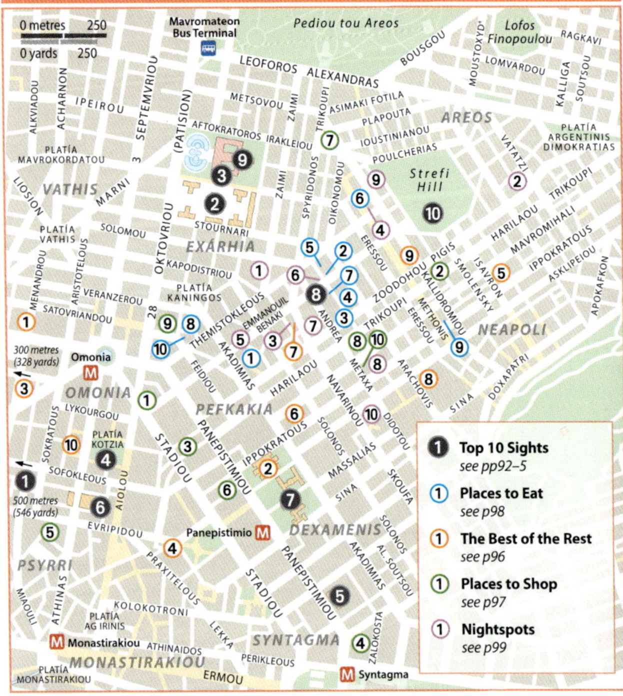

Bronze statue at the Polytechnic

2 Polytechnic

MAP C/D1–2

The Polytechnic is where the student protests against the junta in 1973 *(see p94)* began. In front, beside the gate that was crushed by the junta's tanks on 17 November 1973, is a monument to those who died in the uprising: a large bronze head resting on the ground. This date is now a national holiday, commemorated every year with parades and protests.

Carved stele, Epigraphical Museum

3 Epigraphical Museum

MAP D1 ■ Tositsa 1 ■ 210 823 2950 ■ Open 8:30am–3pm Wed–Mon

Housed here is a fascinating trove of Athenean lore. The collection comprises over 14,000, mostly Greek, inscriptions. The most important exhibits include a decree by the assembly of Athens ordering the evacuation of the city before the Persian invasion in 480 BCE; a sacred law concerning temple-worship on the Acropolis; and a stele carved with accounts of the construction of the Erechtheion at the Acropolis in 421 BCE.

4 Platía Kotzia

MAP C3

Lined with beautiful Neo-Classical buildings, this square is home to the Athens City Hall and the headquarters of the National Bank of Greece. Next door to the bank is the more contemporary National Bank of Greece Cultural Centre, which was cleverly built to show off the remains of the ancient Acharnian Gate. Look out for the antiquities that were uncovered in the square, including tombs and part of an ancient road that once led out of the city.

5 Numismatic Museum of Athens

MAP M2 ■ El Venizelou 12 ■ 210 363 2057 ■ Open 8:30am–3:30pm Wed–Mon (Apr–Oct: 9am–7pm Thu) ■ Adm

Selections from a vast collection of over 500,000 acquisitions chronicle history from 14th century BCE to the present. Aside from the displays of coins, medals, stamps, bank notes and related objects, the setting is spectacular; the sumptuous Iliou Melathron ("Palace of Troy") was built by Ernst Ziller for the archaeologist Heinrich Schliemann, who excavated Troy and Mycenae.

Ancient Greek coins displayed at the Numismatic Museum of Athens

Nut stall, Varvakios Central Market

17 NOVEMBER 1973

The 1973 students of the Polytechnic are hailed as brave role models in the modern Greek state. In November 1973, they demonstrated against the junta, which had been in power since 1967. On 17 November, the uprising was crushed with tanks and guns but their valour contributed to the junta's fall and Greece's liberation the following year.

6 Varvakios Central Market

MAP K1/2 ■ Open 7am–3pm Mon–Sat

The enormous meat, fish and spice markets are a sensory overload that shouldn't be missed by any but the most squeamish. Several restaurants dot the meat market. Outside, the air around the spice stores, centred on Athinas, is redolent with oregano, thyme and dried mountain sage tea.

7 Academy of Athens

MAP L/M1–2 ■ Panepistimiou

The city's university, the Academy of Athens and the National Library *(see p96)* make up a trio of the most important Neo-Classical buildings in Athens. The column bases and capitals of the university entrance are replicas of those in the Acropolis Propylaia, and the Academy entrance draws from the eastern side of the Erechtheion. The university's frescoes depict King Otto surrounded by personifications of the arts.

8 Benaki, Valtetsiou and Kallidromiou

Decidedly Athens' most sociable, engaged and politically charged neighbourhood, Exárhia is where Athenians congregate to enjoy lively intellectual debate with friends over meze and a carafe of raki. You can also visit art house cinemas, and shop for cultural essentials at the many publishing houses, musical instrument workshops, record stores, design labs and studios. The main thoroughfares of Benaki, Valtetsiou, Kallidromiou and the surrounding streets are

Sprawling campus of the Academy of Athens

filled with fantastic street art and enchantingly casual places to eat, drink and enjoy the flow of conversation filling the streets until the late hours, every day of the week.

9 National Archaeological Museum

This superb museum, often known simply as the National Museum *(see pp20–21)*, opened in 1891, bringing together a collection that had previously been scattered across the city. With its unique exhibits, including an unrivalled amount of Ancient Greek sculpture, pottery and jewelley, this is without doubt one of the finest museums in the world.

Aedusa at the National Museum

10 Strefi Hill (Lofos Strefis)

MAP E1 ■ Anexartisias & :mmanouil Benaki

;trefi Hill is often overlooked by 'isitors due to its reputation as an ınpleasant hangout by night. How- :ver, the hill is perfectly safe to visit luring the day, where a short hike akes you up to a vantage point (tread ery carefully as the path isn't paved) vith spectacular views of the gritty eighbourhoods of Omonia, Exárhia, ne Lykavittos Hill, the Acropolis nd beyond. It is recommended ıat visitors leave before dark.

A DAY AROUND OMONIA

MORNING

Start at Greece's greatest treasure storehouse: the **National Archaeological Museum**. Don't miss the Mycenean Treasure, Thera Frescoes and Classical statuary.

When leaving the museum, turn left on Patission, noting the nearby **Polytechnic** *(see p93)*, scene of 1973's historic protests. Outside the building, a giant bronze head and a crushed gate lie on the ground, a memorial to the fallen students.

Turn left on **Stournari**, and make your way to **Valtetsiou Street**, above Platía Exárhia, for a frappé. In summer, head to **Yiantes** *(see p98)* for an alfresco lunch.

AFTERNOON

Travel downhill on Themistokleous. Walk quickly past the historic but chaotic **Platía Omonia** on **Athinas**. Once beyond here you'll pass the stately **Athens City Hall** *(see p96)* on your right before turning left onto Sofokleous. Go down this street to see the **National Bank of Greece**, built on stilts over part of the Themistoklean Wall. Across Aiolou, the archaeological digs lie exposed.

Double back to get to the city's real heart – the **Varvakios Central Market**. Lose yourself in the sights, sounds and smells of the stalls. Just one market taverna has survived the economic crisis: **Epirus**, famous for its *patsas* (tripe soup), the classic Greek hangover cure.

See map on p92

The Best of the Rest

1 National Theatre

MAP B2 ■ Agiou Konstantinou 22–4 ■ 210 528 8170 ■ www.n-t.gr/en

The majestic outlines of Hadrian's Library served as the model for this fine Neo-Classical building's façade. Performances by the National Theatre troupe are Greece's best.

National Library

2 National Library

MAP L1 ■ Panepistimiou 32 ■ www.nlg.gr

The National Library has moved to the Stavros Niarchos Foundation Cultural Centre, but Theophil Hansen's original building – part of his famous trilogy with the university and Academy of Athens *(see p94)* – continues to define Athenian Neo-Classical elegance.

3 Rebecca Camhi Gallery

MAP B2 ■ Leonidou 9 ■ Open noon–6pm Tue–Thu, noon–9pm Fri, noon–4pm Sat ■ www.rebeccacamhi.com

This gallery presents both Greek and foreign contemporary artists.

4 Agii Theodoroi

MAP K2 ■ Plateia Agion Theodoron

A tiny, peaceful 11th-century church in the bustle of the marketplace. The wall paintings are 19th century.

5 CHEAPART Athens

MAP D2 ■ Andrea Metaxa 25 ■ www.cheapart.gr

A not-for-profit art space that hosts exhibitions by contemporary Greek, international and emerging artists.

6 Loverdos Museum – Ziller Mansion

MAP D3 ■ Mavromichali 6 ■ Open 8:30am–3:30pm Wed–Mon

In the mansion of Athens' premier Neo-Classicist Ernst Ziller *(see p102)*, you can enjoy the fabulous Loverdos collection of Byzantine Art alongside the building's beautiful architecture.

7 Grigoropoulos Shrine

MAP D2 ■ Tzavella

Teenager Alexandros Grigoropoulos was shot by the police in December 2008. Three days of riots ensued. A plaque, flowers and candles are dedicated to him.

8 Athens City Hall

MAP J1 ■ Athinas 63

The headquarters for managing Greater Athens' 40 municipalities. The archaeological dig in front reveals an area just outside Athens' old city walls.

9 Odos Kallidromiou

MAP D2

The colourful Saturday "*laiki*", the weekly farmers' market, on this street provides a real feel of the vibrant Exárhia community.

10 Agios Nikolaos Pefkakia

MAP E2 ■ Asklipeiou

Built in 1895, the church of St Nicholas of the Pines crowns the top of steep Dervenion Street.

Church of Agios Nikolaos Pefkakia

Places to Shop

Interior of Naked Summers

1 Miran
MAP K2 ■ Evripidou 45

Set up by Armenian refugees in 1922, this shop offers fantastic *pastourma* (cured veal or camel) and *soutzouki* (spicy veal salami).

2 Nikolaos Germanos Shoes
MAP E2 ■ Kallidromiou 24 ■ 693 662 1021

Footwear designer Nikolaos Germanos from the Athens School of Fine Arts and St. Martin's creates whimsical, wearable works of art in this studio in Exarchia.

3 Stoa tou Vivliou
MAP C3 ■ Pesmazoglou 5 & Stadiou

In the commercial heart of Athens, this tranquil arcade with old-world charm houses bookshops, binders and antiquarian outlets.

4 Zoumboulakis Gallery
MAP M3 ■ Kriezotou 6 ■ www.zoumboulakis.gr

This celebrated art gallery and shop has a spectacular selection of original paintings and signed, numbered prints by many of Greece's finest artists.

5 Politeia
MAP D2 ■ Asklipiou 1–3 ■ www.politeianet.gr

A highly revered and well-curated bookshop with a great section of books in English.

6 Xylouris
MAP L1 ■ Stoa Pesmazoglou, Panepistimiou 39

Named after the late singer Nikos Xylouris, this store is a treasure house of traditional Greek music and rare CDs.

7 Yesterday's Bread
MAP D1 ■ Ioustinianou 2 ■ 210 881 1233

This vintage clothing boutique is an integral part of the Exárhia community and the ideal place to up your look with decades of sustainable style.

8 Organopoieion
MAP D3 ■ Didotou 38

A workshop for handcrafted, made-to-order traditional Greek musical instruments – truly works of art.

Bouzoukia on sale in a store

9 Mimi's Sunglasses
MAP C2 ■ Gladstonos 2

This family-run shop has specialized in sunglasses since 1962, and carries a range of affordable retro-chic styles.

10 Naked Summers
MAP D2 ■ Didotou 30 ■ www.nakedsummers.com

Artist Christina Mandilari crafts ceramics and accessories with poetic and playful designs that capture the Mediterranean summer.

See map on p92

Places to Eat

1 Tivoli

MAP D2 ■ Emmanouil Benaki 34 ■ 210 383 0919 ■ €

This *mezedopolio* is also a live music venue. It offers regional dishes from Skopelos and affordable drinks.

2 Klimataria

MAP J1 ■ Platía Theatrou 2 ■ 210 321 6629 ■ €

This warm, old-world taverna in Omonia is known for its acoustic rembetika music.

Dining at Klimataria taverna

3 Salero

MAP D2 ■ Valtetsiou 51 ■ 210 381 3358 ■ €

Open until 2am, this place serves Mediterranean tapas, cheese platters and desserts.

4 Yiantes

MAP D2 ■ Valtetsiou 44 ■ 210 330 1369 ■ €

Exárhia's poshest taverna offers creative versions of Greek and Mediterranean dishes. The ingredients used to prepare the dishes are produced organically.

PRICE CATEGORIES

For a three-course meal for one with half a bottle of wine (or equivalent meal), taxes and extra charges.

€ under €40 €€ €40–€60 €€€ over €60

5 Rozalia

MAP D2 ■ Valtetsiou 59 ■ 210 380 2725 ■ €

Waiters present a giant tray of *mezedes* (small plates) to choose from. They also offer outdoor seating in the courtyard during summers.

6 Ama Lachei

MAP D1 ■ Kallidromiou 69, Athina 106 83 ■ 210 384 5978 ■ €

Set in an old schoolyard, this place has a lovely garden. Wash down the food with raki served by the carafe.

7 Oxo Nou

MAP D2 ■ 106 81, Emmanouil Benaki 63 ■ 210 380 1778 ■ €

Cretan cuisine shines at this lively corner in Exárhia with superb *staka*, *cochilous*, *boureki* and more.

8 I Kriti

MAP C2 ■ Veranzerou 5 ■ €

Set in an arcade this place serves up Cretan platters and sausages, along with Sitian wine.

9 Tanini Agapi Mou

MAP D2 ■ 91 Ippokratous & Methonis ■ €

Try Greece's organic, natural and biodynamic wines plus expert light fare at "Tannin, my love".

10 Stoa Allios

MAP C2 ■ Gamveta 14 ■ 210 382 5961 ■ €

Marvellous seafood, fresh fish, lovely salads, classic sides and very good prices distinguish this clean, cheerful neighbourhood taverna.

Nightspots

The rock band Biohazard performing at An Club

1 An Club

MAP C2 ■ Solomou 13–15 ■ www.anclub.gr

One of Athens' oldest and best-loved venues for live music, An Club showcases rock and alternative bands. Check the website for the event schedule.

2 Makari

MAP E1 ■ Zoodochou Pigis 125 & Komninon ■ 210 645 8958

This bar hosts acoustic sets and rembetika, as well as theatre performances, poetry readings and other events in an atmospheric space.

3 Beatniks Road Bar

MAP D2 ■ Koletti 14

Enjoy DJd, live blues and rock music at this bar. The walls are decorated with various homages to beatnik, early rock and jazz culture.

4 Efimeron

MAP D2 ■ Methonis 58 ■ 210 384 1848

Located on a quiet back street, this excellent taverna offers a varied menu. Many nights there's also live rembetika.

5 Tivoli Live

MAP D2 ■ Emmanouil Benaki 34 ■ 210 383 0919

Established rembetika stars perform here. Book in advance as there are limited seats.

6 Alexandrino

MAP D2 ■ Emmanouil Benaki 69 A

A local favourite, this small café-bistro is famous for its excellent wines and cocktails as well as teas.

7 Off The Chain

MAP D2 ■ Zoödohou Pigis 25

This bar plays alternative rock, indie and industrial music. It fills up late (after 3am) and parties till sunrise at weekends.

8 Lulu Athens

MAP D2 ■ Ippokratous 59 ■ 210 363 9355

This place offers a classic cocktail menu and delicious daiquiris, plus bruschetta and good bar snacks.

9 Enikos

MAP D1 ■ Kallidromiou 57, Athina

Popular with artists and writers, this cosy place at the edge of Exárhia is ideal for drinks and good conversation – lively but not too loud.

10 Ippopotamus

MAP D3 ■ Delfon ■ 210 363 4583

Set on a pretty tree-lined alley leading to Kolonaki, this charming café is a local favourite. There is plenty of outdoor seating with tables spilling onto the streets. It is the perfect spot to grab a drink.

See map on p92

TOP 10 Syntagma and Kolonaki

Plateia Syntagma, the centre of modern Athens, is crowned by the large, Neo-Classical Parliament Building. Standing sentry outside are the *evzones* (soldiers) marching solemnly in traditional kilts and *tsarouhia* (pompommed shoes). Extending from the left side of the Parliament Building is the grand Vasilissis Sofias avenue, lined with embassies and several of Athens' finest museums. Beyond Vasilissis Sofias lies posh Kolonaki, home to ambassadors, politicians and celebrities – and to the fabulous designer boutiques that cater to them. This is the prime spot for shopping, people-watching and pricey café-sitting. Rising above it all is Lykavittos Hill, topped by a famous outdoor theatre, cafés and a restaurant with views out to Piraeus.

***Evzone* guard in traditional attire**

SYNTAGMA AND KOLONAKI

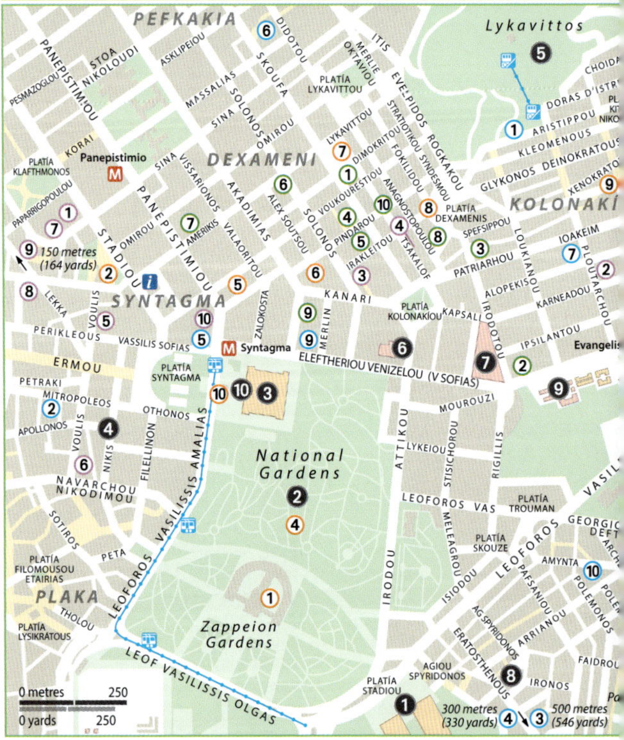

1 Kallimarmaro Stadium

MAP N6 ■ Vas Konstantinou ■ Open 8am–7pm daily (Nov–Feb: to 5pm) ■ www.panathenaicstadium.gr

Also known as the Panathenaic, the Kallimarmaro (meaning "beautiful marble", *see p61*) was built in 330 BCE for the Panathenaic games. In 1895, George Averoff had it restored with fine Pentelic marble ahead of the first modern Olympics in 1896. In 2004, the stadium provided the final circuit for the Olympic Marathon and hosted the archery competition. It is still used for concerts and other events, and is open to runners on most mornings.

2 National Gardens

MAP M4 ■ Amalias

The huge, shady National Gardens are an unexpected green refuge in parched central Athens. They were originally planted in 1839 as the Royal Garden of Queen Amalia, who had her horticulturalists (and the Greek fleet) bring in 15,000 domestic plants, many of which are still alive. The garden was opened to the public in 1923. It has a shady café in the northeast corner, two duck ponds, free-ranging tortoises and a playground.

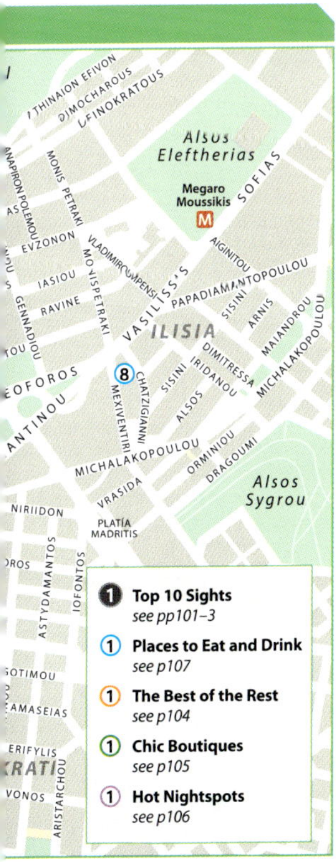

3 National Parliament Building

MAP M3 ■ Platía Syntagma ■ Library: Open 9am–2pm & 5:30–8:30pm Mon–Fri, 9am–2pm Sat ■ www.hellenicparliament.gr

This grand building was originally built in 1842 as a palace for King Otto. Over the next 70 years, it suffered neglect, and in 1923, it served as a shelter for refugees from Asia Minor. In 1926, after the return of parliamentary government, the building was rebuilt and re-opened as a single-chamber council for parliament. Free guided tours can be arranged 15 days in advance.

National Parliament Building

4 Syntagma Metro Station

MAP M3

Syntagma metro station is as much museum as transport hub. When the city was busy excavating to extend the metro, archaeologists found thousands of priceless items on this site, which has been continuously occupied since Classical times. Many are displayed in the station, but the highlight is a glass wall overlooking the site, which includes at least two cemeteries.

Lykavittos Hill and the neighbourhood of Kolonaki

5 Lykavittos Hill
MAP F2

Steep Lykavittos Hill juts high out of Kolonaki, and the church at its peak is visible for miles around. Every summer, the Lykavittos Festival hosts a variety of top musicians from around the world in the theatre beyond the church; there's nothing like watching Bob Dylan with the sun going down over Athens behind them. A smart café-restaurant nestles below the church. If you are very, very ambitious, walk up – otherwise, take the funicular from Aristippou.

ERNST ZILLER

Shortly after the Kingdom of Greece was established in 1832, Neo-Classicism became the dominant architectural style in Athens. Ernst Ziller was its foremost practitioner, who designed more than 500 buildings across Greece. His Athens masterpieces include the Museum of Cycladic Art, the Numismatic Museum *(see p104)* and his own mansion, which is now the Loverdos Museum *(see p96)*.

6 Benaki Museum of Greek Culture

The Benaki *(see pp26–7)* is one of Greece's pre-eminent museums, not only for its extensive and impressive collection of prehistoric to 20th-century Greek art, but also because it's a lovely place to be. Among its highlights are the re-creations of Ottoman-style sitting rooms in 18th-century northern Greek mansions, and Byzantine shrines. The superb books and jewellery in the gift shop and the rooftop garden restaurant are destinations in themselves.

Icon of The Raising of Lazaros, Benaki Museum of Greek Culture

7 Museum of Cycladic Art

Some 2,000 years before the Parthenon, a mysterious civilization on the Cycladic islands created the prototypical Mediterranean marble sculptures: simple, and mostly elemental female forms. The figures still resonate today, famously influencing artists such as Modigliani, Moore and Picasso *(see pp22–3)*. The Goulandris family, one of Greece's oldest shipping and philanthropic dynasties, displays the world's largest collection of Cycladic art in a building erected in 1985 by the architect Ioannis Vikelas. There are often exhibits by top contemporary Greek and international artists in the extra-swanky exhibition wing.

8 Basil and Elise Goulandris Foundation

MAP P5 ■ Eratosthenous 13 ■ 210 725 2895 ■ Open 10am–6pm Wed–Mon (to 8pm Fri) ■ Adm ■ www.goulandris.gr

This collection of modern and contemporary art features works by masters of the European avant-garde, as well as pieces by modern Greek artists such as Chryssa, Takis, Ghikas, Tsarouchis and the contemporary master Rorris. The beautifully lit works are hung in a fine four-storey space designed by architect I M Pei.

9 Byzantine and Christian Museum

The museum's *(see pp32–3)* collection dates from the 3rd to the 19th centuries, chronicling the rise and fall of the Byzantine Empire and its influence on the areas which would become Greece. It is housed in a two-level space built partially under ground.

Byzantine and Christian Museum

10 Evzones

MAP M3 ■ Changing of the Guard every hour

On guard in front of Parliament are the famous *evzones*, soldiers in the traditional attire of the rebels who won the War of Independence. It's hard to imagine fighting efficiently in this uniform: a short white skirt with 400 pleats, symbolizing the years under Ottoman rule), red cap and *tsarouhia* (pompommed shoes). The Changing of the Guard is like a slow high-kick dance. *Evzones* are selected from the men in the mandatory Greek military service. The best time to watch is on Sunday, at 11am in the morning.

AN AFTERNOON IN CHIC KOLONAKI

MID-AFTERNOON

Start at **Platía Syntagma** a few minutes before the hour to see the Changing of the Guard in front of the **Tomb of the Unknown Soldier**. Then head up **Vasilissis Sofias** to the **Museum of Cycladic Art** to ponder the mysterious prehistoric marble sculptures. Check out whatever temporary exhibition is on at the adjoining Stathatos Mansion – they are usually world-class shows.

Then it's on to **Platía Kolonakiou** for a freddo espresso and a pastry at one of the cafés along the Tsakalof pedestrian way. After a relaxing sit down and some people-watching, enjoy a little window-shopping.

LATE AFTERNOON

For lunch, head to **Taverna Filippou** at Xenokratous 19. After lunch, fan out from the square to take in the cosmopolitan street scene and enjoy browsing for unique finds at shops like **Parthenis** and **Sophia** *(see p105)*, as well as familiar international staples such as Dior, Prada and Balenciaga.

Towards the end of the day, go to the **Funicular Station** at the foot of **Lykavittos Hill**. From the hilltop at dusk, watch the sky turn violet over Athens, while enjoying a drink at the café, or a truly memorable meal at **Orizontes** restaurant *(see p107)*.

See map on pp100–101

The Best of the Rest

1 Zappeion

MAP M5

The Zappeion designed by Theophil Hansen in 1874, stands in pleasant grounds at the southern end of the National Gardens. Its tree-lined paths are open to the public, while the Zappeion itself hosts various events.

National Historical Museum

2 National Historical Museum

MAP L2 ■ Stadiou 13, Platîa Kolokotroni ■ Open 9am–4pm Tue–Sun ■ Adm ■ www.nhmuseum.gr

In Greece's first parliament building, educational displays track the city's history from the fall of Byzantium Empire to Latin and Ottoman rule, the National Awakening of the 18th century, and then the revolution and eventful decades that followed.

3 Gennadeion Library

MAP F3 ■ Souidias 61 ■ Open 9am–4:45pm Mon–Fri, 9am–1:45pm Sat ■ www.ascsa.edu.gr

Now part of the American School of Classical Studies, this library of multilingual volumes is one of the world's best resources for all things Hellenic.

4 Presidential Palace

MAP N4 ■ Between Irodou Attikou & Meleagrou

The former palace of King Constantine I was designed by Ernst Ziller *(see p102)* from 1891–97.

5 Ghika Gallery

MAP M2 ■ Kriezotou 3 ■ Open 10am–6pm Sat & Sun ■ Adm

Greek painter Nikos Ghika's studio highlights 20th-century Greek poetry, theatre, music and architecture.

6 Kotsanas Museum

MAP D4 ■ Pindarou 6 ■ Open 10am–6pm daily ■ www. kotsanas museum.com

An ode to Ancient Greek technology, this museum houses around 300 operating models of their inventions.

7 Church of St Dionysius the Areopagite

MAP E3 ■ Skoufa 34 ■ 210 3613436 ■ Open 7:30am–7:30pm daily

This church has stunning interiors painted by Spyros Vassiliou, one of Greece's leading modern artist.

8 Platía Dexameni

MAP N/P2

Home to a popular café and meze place, plus an outdoor cinema.

9 Friday Morning Street Market

MAP P2 ■ Xenokratous

This is one of Athens' most lively outdoor fruit and vegetable markets.

10 Tomb of the Unknown Soldier

MAP M3 ■ Platía Syntagma

A relief carving of a dying gunner, made by sculptor Fokion Rok in 1930-32, adorns this cenotaph honouring independent Greece's war dead.

Tomb of the Unknown Soldier

Chic Boutiques

Colourful interior of the Benaki Museum' shop

1 Parthenis

MAP N2 ■ Dimokritou 20 ■ 21 0363 3158

Shop for elegant, casual clothing in urban and island Greek styles.

2 Dassios

MAP P3 ■ Vasilissis Sofias 35 ■ www.dassios.com

Dimitris Dassios creates extravagant but tasteful denim-wear, jackets, bags and jewellery from silk and leather, with ornamental details.

3 Oikos

MAP E4 ■ Irodotou 26 ■ www.oikos.gr

The most contemporary designs in Greece are showcased at this expensive store selling furniture, lighting and accessories.

4 Sophia

MAP N2 ■ Pindarou 15, Athina 106 73 ■ 210 360 6930

Sophia – "wisdom" in Greek – has a delightful mix of playful yet useful objects with a philosophical touch and pop sensibility, plus inspiring books and games and clever housewares.

5 Heel Athens Lab

Iraklitou 11 ■ 210 361 6286

Inventive, relaxed street fashion, made from organic cotton in unisex styles – ethical, sustainable and conscientious.

6 Benaki Museum Shop

MAP N2 ■ Koumpari 1, Athina 106 74 ■ www.benakishop.gr

An outstanding selection of museum replicas, including wonderful jewellery pieces, plus contemporary creations made with care by artisans using traditional techniques.

7 Kombologadiko

Amerikis 9 ■ 212 700 0500

This is the place for traditional Greek rosary beads crafted from amber, wood and semi-precious stones.

8 Elena Votsi

MAP N/P2 ■ Xanthou 7 ■ www.elenavotsi.gr

A popular name on the international jewellery circuit, Votsi does chunky, rough-edged investment pieces.

9 Vassilis Zoulias

MAP D4 ■ Akadimias 4 ■ 210 722 5613

This popular haute-couture boutique embodies the elegance of times past, and crafts glamorous, made-to-order clothing pieces.

10 Mr. Vertigo

Pl Filikis Eterias 15 ■ www.mrvertigo.wine

Natural and biodynamic Greek wines as well as those from indigenous grape varieties are a speciality at this store.

See map on pp100–101

Nightspots

Seating area of the elegant Oinoscent wine bar

1 Mingus Cava Bar

MAP D3 ■ Skoufa 52

Sample an eclectic choice of wine and cocktails as you hum along to live music at this initmate bar. Knowledgeable staff are on hand to help you make the perfect choice.

2 Mai Tai AΘens

MAP P3 ■ Ploutarchou 18

The friendly staff serve delicious classic cocktails with a twist at this pleasant bar, which attracts a fashionable clientele.

3 Alexander's Bar

MAP D4 ■ Vasileos Georgiou A, Syntagma Square

A clubby, classic bar at the historic Grande Bretagne hotel, this is the most elegant room in the city, with excellent drinks and live piano in the evenings.

4 Minnie the Moocher

MAP N2 ■ Tsakalof 6

Set on Kolonaki's posh pedestrian strip, this 1930s-style hotspot serves a range of great cocktails, with jazz and swing music often playing.

5 Seven Jokers

MAP L4 ■ Voulis 7

This café-bar aims to re-create the atmosphere of 1920s Paris. Huge sandwiches help to absorb the vast amounts of alcohol served.

6 Oinoscent

MAP D4 ■ Voulis 45

Enjoy a superb selection of Greek and international wines by the glass, expertly curated tastings. Expect excellent food here.

7 Rock 'n' Roll

MAP E4 ■ Loukianou 6

An old Kolonaki favourite, this bar operates out of its original 1987 location. Enjoy the atmosphere set by a classic rock playlist and a slightly older crowd.

8 Drunk Sinatra

MAP L3 ■ Thiseos 16

This colourful and trendy vintage bar hosts a lively crowd that often spills out onto the pedestrian street.

9 The Clumsies

MAP K2 ■ Praxitelous 30

Set in a Neo-Classical mansion from 1919, this popular bar with a wooden beamed ceiling and striking decor serves great cocktails, light snacks and Sunday brunch.

10 Milioni Street

MAP N3

This street's fairy lights attract the youth of Kolonaki until the early hours, as do the many other bars and cafés.

Places to Eat and Drink

PRICE CATEGORIES
For a three-course meal for one with half a bottle of wine (or equivalent meal), taxes and extra charges.

€ under €40 €€ €40–€60 €€€ over €60

1 Café Merlin

MAP D4 ■ Vasilissis Sofias 9, at Merlin ■ 210 361 1731 ■ €

At the B&M Theocharakis Institute, this cultured oasis in the city centre has a contemporary Mediterranean menu and a great brunch selection.

2 Ergon House Athens

MAP C4 ■ Mitropoleos Street 23, Athina 105 57 ■ 210 010 9090 ■ €

Inventive and original Greek dishes and top artisanal ingredients in a bright, convivial atrium.

3 Spondi

MAP E6 ■ Pyrronos 5 ■ 210 756 4021 ■ €€€

Upmarket French cuisine with Greek references – think crab, langoustine and milk-fed lamb. Only dinner is served.

4 Mouries

MAP E6 ■ Platia Varnava and Krisila, Pangrati ■ 210 701 6100 ■ €

For a specialist in *magirefta* (casserole dishes), head to Mouries, especially for lunch. Tables are set inside and out, under namesake mulberries.

5 Winter Garden

MAP M3 ■ Vasileos Georgiou 1, Platia Syntagma ■ 210 333 0000 ■ €€€

Enjoy a European breakfast, lunch, high tea or dinner at this restaurant in the luxurious Hotel Grande Bretagne.

6 Il Postino

MAP D3 ■ Griveon 3, off Skoufa ■ 210 364 1414 ■ €

This genuine, Italian-run *osteria* serves pasta dishes (20 choices daily), salads and a few heartier mains, plus of course tiramisu, in a very quiet setting.

7 Oikeio

MAP E4 ■ Plutarchou 15 ■ 210 725 9216 ■ €€

This bistro with objet-trouve decor has all the Greek staples including less common ones such as sauteed rabbit. Reservations are suggested; service is friendly.

8 Cookoovaya

MAP F4 ■ Hatzigianni Mexi 2a ■ 210 723 5005 ■ €€€

The daily changing menu here offers salads, grilled grouper with orzo, fennel and botarga, or fresh hake with artichokes, beans, peas and fennel.

Al-fresco dining at Orizontes

9 Orizontes

MAP P1 ■ Aristippou 1 ■ 210 721 0701 ■ €€€

Enjoy a view of the capital stretching to the Saronic Gulf while dining on creative Greek cuisine and risotto/pasta dishes atop Lykavittos Hill.

10 Akra

MAP F5 ■ Aminta 12, Pangrati ■ 210 725 1116 ■ €€

Conscientiously sourced ingredients are crafted into insightful, creative dishes at Akra. Try the delicious creations of one of the best pastry chefs in the city here.

See map on pp100–101

TOP 10 Piraeus

Integral to the Athenian experience, Piraeus – the Mediterranean's third largest port – is truly a city unto itself. Greece's seafaring identity finds its fullest expression here, and the essential connection to the islands is deeply felt amid a sea of passengers, trucks and cranes. Luxury yachts and fine dining in the Pasalimani show its glamorous side, while hillside Neo-Classical Kastella and the Mikrolimano with its fishing boats capture its traditional character.

Hellenic Maritime Museum

1 Hellenic Maritime Museum

Akti Themistokleous, Freattyda ■ Open 9am–2pm Tue–Sat ■ Adm ■ www.hmmuseum.gr

Housed in a 1960s building at the mouth of Zea Marina, this exhibition opens with a map of Odysseus's voyage across the Mediterranean. It then traces the history of Greek naval trading, with models of ships ranging

PIRAEUS

from the 5th-century BCE trireme *(see p54)* to modern tankers (Greece has the largest merchant fleet in the world). Naval warfare is covered by massive oil paintings of historic sea battles against the Ottomans.

Walking along Flisvos Marina

2 Zea (Pasalimani)

This large bay, with a bottleneck channel opening out to the sea, is surrounded by tall apartment blocks. Inaugurated as Athens' main naval base in the 5th century BCE, the ancient harbour of Marina Zea could accommodate 196 triremes. Today, up to 400 of the most impressive motor yachts in Greece moor here. It takes about 20 minutes to walk the perimeter of the bay, along a tree-lined promenade overlooked by tavernas and cafés.

3 Flisvos Marina

Tram to Trocadero or Parko Flisvou

Perfect for families, the marina has a promenade, parks and playgrounds. Take a morning stroll on the beach before enjoying a dip in the sea just to the south; here there are also plenty of cafés and restaurants. There's also an outdoor cinema in summer.

4 Archaeological Museum of Piraeus

Harilaou Trikoupi 31 ■ 210 452 1598 ■ Open Apr–Oct: 9am–5pm Wed–Mon; Nov–Mar: 8:30am–3:30pm Wed–Mon ■ Adm

Built beside the remains of the 2nd-century BCE Theatre of Zea, the showpieces here are two classical bronze statues: the perfectly proportioned 5th-century BCE Piraeus Apollo and the 4th-century BCE Piraeus Athena. Also on display is a collection of 5th- and 4th-century BCE marble *stelai* (Classical gravestones) with reliefs of the deceased.

Archaeological Museum of Piraeus

5 Akti Themistokleous

From Freattyda, a 3-km- (2-mile-) long coastal promenade, overlooked by apartment blocks and a string of informal fish restaurants, offers wonderful views across the open sea to the islands of Egina and Salamina. The route, named after the 5th-century BCE general and statesman Themistokles, who founded Piraeus, follows the course of the ancient seaward walls. Down below, a series of rocky bays offers sunbathing. The prettiest spot of all is Aphrodite's Bay.

6 Kastella

Built into the northern and eastern sides of the Profitis Ilias hill, which overlooks Mikrolimano, this residential quarter is filled with pastel-coloured Neo-Classical houses, built between 1834 and 1900, and a labyrinth of steep streets and stairways. There's a village atmosphere here, making it a great area to explore on foot. The highest point is crowned by the church of Profitis Ilias, which offers spectacular views of Athens, while on the southern slope the small open-air Veakeio Theatre is used for staging summer performances.

7 Yacht Club of Greece

Mikrolimano

Europe's top destination for yachters, thanks to its myriad islands, Greece has a 3,500-year tradition of sailing.

Yacht Club of Greece

Mikrolimano's bay

Set in landscaped gardens on a peninsula on the south side of Mikrolimano, the yacht club was founded in 1934. The main clubhouse is the province of members only, but you can stroll around the marina, then stop for a drink at the chic rooftop bar, Istioploïkos *(see p113)*.

Battleship Averof

8 Battleship Averof

Flisvos Marina, Trokadero, Paleo Faliro ■ 210 988 8211 ■ Open 9am–2pm Tue–Fri, 10am–5pm Sat & Sun ■ Adm

Built in Livorno (Italy) in 1910, this 140-m- (460-ft-) long battleship was designed to carry 670 men in peacetime and 1,200 during war, and led the Greek fleet through the Balkan Wars and World Wars I and II. Negotiating a series of narrow ladders, you can explore the entire ship, from the kitchen and engine rooms to the main bridge, from the cramped dark space where the crew slept in hammocks, to the contrasting luxury of the officers' mess and the Admiral's sumptuous wood-panelled suite.

9 Mikrolimano

Known for its fish restaurants with open-air waterside terraces, this circular bay is built on a human scale. The ancients believed it was protected by the goddess Artemis, and initially named it after the Mounihia festival. The Ottoman navy used it too, which is why it is still sometimes known as Tourkolimano (Turkish harbour). Today it is filled with the small wooden boats of local fishers, who supply the surrounding restaurants from their daily catch.

10 Stavros Niarchos Foundation Cultural Center (SNFCC)

Syggrou Avenue 364 at Poseidonos T7 to Tzitziphies ■ www.snfcc.org

The SNFCC is a public space, which hosts a range of cultural, educational, athletic, environmental and recreational events. It is home to the Greek National Opera, the National Library of Greece and the Stavros Niarchos Park. Designed by Renzo Piano, the complex has a lighthouse, which offers views of Athens, Piraeus and the Saronic Gulf.

LION OF PIRAEUS

In medieval times the main port of Piraeus was known as Porto Leone in tribute to a 3-m- (10-ft-) tall marble lion that stood on the site of the present Town Hall. In 1687, the Venetians carried it off and placed it in the Arsenale in Venice. A copy of the original stands on Akti Favierou, visible from approaching ferries.

A DAY IN PIRAEUS

MORNING/AFTERNOON

From Athens, take the metro to Piraeus, then walk to the **Archaeological Museum** *(see p109)* and check out some of the ancient local finds.

Continue to **Zea (Pasalimani)** and stop for a coffee at **Moby** *(see p113)*, overlooking the water. Take the time for a stroll around the harbour to admire the top-notch boats.

For a relaxed lunch, call at **Imerovigli** *(see p112)*, which offers fantastic sea views; otherwise, walk the seafront promenade of **Akti Themistokleous** for a reasonably priced informal feast of fresh fish at **Margaro** *(see p112)*.

EVENING

Take the tram T7 to **Flisvos Marina** *(see p107)* to see the historic **Battleship Averoff**. Walk along the promenade and admire the glamorous yachts or savour a post-lunch freddo espresso.

As dusk approaches, it's the perfect time to visit the **Stavros Niarchos Foundation Cultural Center (SNFCC)**. Once you're here, take the elevator all the way up to the lighthouse to marvel at the panoramic views of Athens, Piraeus and the Saronic Gulf.

Dinner options near here range from casual canal-side dining to the two Michelin-starred **Delta** *(www.deltarestaurant.gr)*. Or, return to the central harbour of Piraeus and end your day with an ouso and some seafood at the charming **Yperokeanio** *(see p112)*.

See map on pp108–9

Places to Eat

PRICE CATEGORIES

For a three-course meal for one with half a bottle of wine (or equivalent meal), taxes and extra charges.

€ under €40 €€ €40–€60 €€€ over €60

1 Varoulko Seaside

Akti Koumoundourou 52, Mikrolimano ■ 210 522 8400 ■ €€€

Michelin-starred chef Lefteris Lazarou serves seafood delights such as squid with pesto, and red mullet in lemon sauce. They offer a tasting menu as well as à la carte.

2 Dourabeis

Akti Dilaveri 29, Mikrolimano ■ 210 412 2092 ■ €€€

Since 1933, Dourabeis has charmed diners with its sublime fresh fish and shellfish, simply grilled and dressed with lemon and olive oil.

3 Jimmy's Fish

Akti Koumoundourou 46, Mikrolimano ■ 210 412 4417 ■ €€€

Expect classic seafood and shellfish appetizers, lobster spaghetti and superb fresh fish – served harborside.

4 Imerovigli

Akti Themistokleous 56, Freattyda ■ 210 452 3382 ■ €

Imerovigli has charming island-style decor and serves excellent seafood, with limited meat choices, accompanied by Greek wines, *ouzo*, *tsipouro* and beers.

5 Falafellas

Karaiskiou 118 ■ 210 323 9809 ■ €

Vegans and vegetarians have plenty of options at this popular, budget-friendly street food spot.

6 Kapilio O Zahos

Komotinis 37, Piraeus ■ 210 481 3325 ■ €

This family-run taverna serves meat and seafood dishes. The interior befits a *kapilio* (wine tavern).

7 Yperokeanio

Marias Chatzikiriakou 48 ■ 210 418 0030 ■ €

With its maritime decor, Yperokeanio (meaning ocean liner) serves classics such as marinated anchovies, steamed mussels and crisp calamari.

8 Margaro

Hatzikyriakou 126 ■ 210 451 4226 ■ Closed Tue & Sun dinner and two weeks in Aug ■ No credit cards ■ €

Diners here enjoy a menu that includes salad, seafood as well as beer or wine. Dishes are prepared with the fresh catch of the day.

9 Papaïoannou

Akti Koumoundourou 42, Mikrolimano ■ 210 422 5059 ■ €€

Noted for its fresh seafood supplied directly from spear-fishers, chef Giorgos Papaïoannou presents creative dishes. The menu includes specialities like sea urchin and crawfish tartare.

10 Stoa Rakadiko

Karaoli & Dimitriou 5, Stoa Kouvelou ■ 210 417 8470 ■ €

With a quirky decor, this place offers some unusual dishes made with buffalo meat. It is an excellent choice before or after a ferry ride.

Vibrant interior of Stoa Rakadiko

Bars and Cafés

Pizza platter at Moby

1 Istioploïkos
Akti Mikrolimano ▪ 210 413 4084 ▪ Open mid-Mar–early Nov

One of the places to see and be seen, this vast rooftop bar commands a vantage point above the yachting marina.

2 Pisina
Akti Themistokleous 25, Freattyda ▪ 210 451 1324

Centred around an open-air swimming pool, this modern bar-restaurant is stylish but relaxed.

3 Rockfellas Excelsior
Marina Zeas ▪ 210 418 4440

With walls covered by posters of well-known musicians, a bar lined with high stools, and leather sofas for lounging on, this place serves draught beer and cocktails. It hosts popular summer parties on Sundays.

4 Stani
Dragatsi 10 ▪ 210 417 4235

A pleasant dairy shop in a small street serving fresh yoghurt, pastries and rice pudding – plus great coffee.

Refreshing Cocktail

5 Paleo
Polidefkous 39 ▪ 210 412 5204

A contemporary wine bar with a Mediterranean menu, set in a beautiful stone building in the Papastratos neighbourhood.

6 Bizz Café Lounge Bar
Akti Koumoundourou 8, Mikrolimano ▪ 210 411 5344

With sofas, pouffes and coffee tables on a wooden deck that goes right up to the water's edge, this place is one of a string of lounge-cafés overlooking Mikrolimano.

7 Moby
Marina Zeas ▪ 211 012 3778

Locals come here for coffee and cocktails, as well as views of the sea. Moby runs DJ nights at weekends, and it serves snacks, pizza and salads, plus Sunday brunch until 3pm.

8 Belle Epoque
Aristotelous 10 ▪ 210 429 7300

Artwork depicting famous fairy-tale characters cover the walls of this café. It opens into the evenings with occasional live music.

9 Filotimos
Agiou Konstantinou 2 ▪ 210 410 0650

Located right next to the Municipal Theatre, this retro-chic bar offers a peaceful escape from the hustle and bustle of the city. Cocktails, tasty small plates and lovely brunch are all available here.

10 Bibere House of Beer
Aggelou Metaxa 5, Pasalimani ▪ 210 411 0004

Greece has a great craft beer culture, with many independent breweries, such as this one. There's a good selection of beers, both local and international, plus a decent food menu. Outdoor seating by the park is a bonus.

See map on pp108–9

TOP 10 North to Delphi

The landscape changes as soon as you reach Athens' northern suburbs; the sight of beautiful Mount Parnitha (often damaged by wildfires) opens the way to the varied landscape of central Greece. The region, Sterea Ellada, is fringed with mountains, lined with coastal towns and dotted with Byzantine monasteries and ancient ruins. Delphi is the country's most beautiful Classical site. Here, the fabled Oracle voiced its prophecies, telling Oedipus, among others, of his terrible fate. Delphi is full of opportunities for swimming, museum-touring and skiing.

Picturesque coastal town of Galaxidi

NORTH TO DELPHI

Ancient temple ruins in Eleusis

1 Ancient Eleusis

MAP S2 ■ 210 554 6019 ■ Bus 876 from Agia Marina metro station ■ Open summer: 8am–8pm Wed–Mon; winter: 8:30am–3:30pm Wed–Mon ■ Adm ■ www.odysseus.culture.gr

For 1,400 years, this was one of Greece's most sacred places. Thousands of pilgrims took part in the Eleusian Mysteries, rites that celebrated Demeter, goddess of nature, and her daughter Persephone.

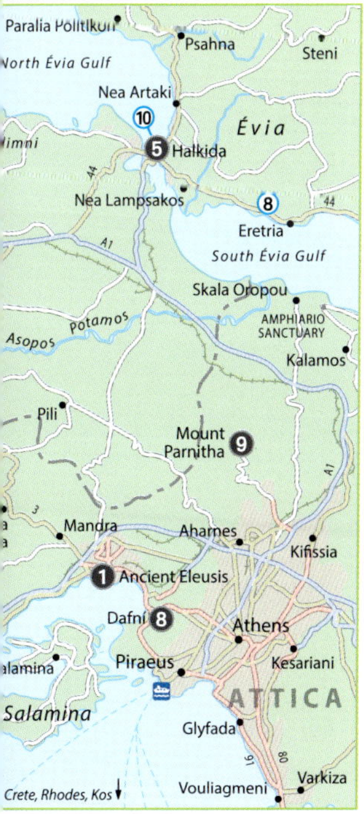

Modern Elefsina is an industrial town and a surprising European Co-Capital of Culture in 2021. There are still some scattered ruins, and an archaeological museum, which is open during the same hours, to help make sense of them.

2 Mount Parnassos

MAP R1 ■ Parnassos Ski Centre ■ www.onparnassos.gr/en

Although developed in parts, Mount Parnassos offers splendid views, fine skiing and, in spring, wonderful trekking over wildflower-covered heights. The highest peak and most popular trek is at 2,457m (8,061 ft) on Liakoura. The truly ambitious can trek via Delphi by starting from Arahova very early in the morning, although this requires a large-scale hiking map. The best commercial product is Anavasi Edition's 1:35,000 Topo 2.1 'Mt Parnassos', most reliably sourced from their Athens shop at Voulis 32, Syntagma.

3 Osios Loukas

MAP R1 ■ 226 702 2797 ■ Open summer: 8:30am–5pm daily; winter: 8am–3pm daily ■ Adm

This is a contender for the most beautiful monastery in Greece, with its idyllic location, looking across a valley to the soaring Elikonas mountain range. The main church, built in 1040, conceals glorious mosaics on the domed ceiling. The crypt has vivid post-Byzantine frescoes.

Ceiling frescoes, Osios Loukas

The mountain village of Arahova

4 Arahova

MAP R1 ■ Several buses daily from Terminal B, stopping en route to Delphi; www.ktel-fokidas.gr

This mountain village makes a good base for visiting Delphi and Parnassos. It is a popular winter destination, though room prices can be higher at this time. The main thoroughfare is lined with shops hawking noodles, wine and cheese. However, the best way to explore is to get lost in its stone-lined passageways.

5 Évia

MAP T1 ■ Halkida tourist office: www.dimoschalkideon.gr/en ■ Bus times and prices: www.ktelevias.gr

Greece's second-largest island is so close to the mainland that you can reach it by bridge. There are several trains a day from Larissa station in Athens to Halkida, Évia's central city. The spine of mountains running north to south and dotted with villages offers great weekend trekking, and if you go by car midweek you'll likely have its beaches and the thermal spas at the northern tip to yourself.

6 Thiva (Thebes)

MAP S2 ■ Buses hourly from Terminal B & several trains daily; www.ktelthivas.gr ■ Museum: Open summer: 8am–7:30pm Wed–Mon; winter: 8:30am–3:30pm Wed–Mon ■ Adm

This city was once one of the greatest Mycenaean settlements and home of the tragic dynasty of Oedipus. Next to nothing remains of the ancient sites, and the modern city offers little in the way of sightseeing, but the town's archaeological museum is worth a visit. It houses artifacts such as the Tanagra figurines.

7 Delphi

MAP Q1

This was considered the centre of the world, as Zeus divined by releasing two eagles from opposite ends of the universe and seeing where they met. Great mystic powers are associated with this site, whose jutting mountain, gaping chasms and rushing springs indicate dramatic geological upheaval. In ancient times, the Pythian priestess presided over the Oracle of Delphi, which gave famously abstruse prophecies. Apollo won dominion over the Oracle by defeating the serpent Python; Apollo's temple *(see p118)* remains the focus of the site.

Temple of Apollo ruins, Delphi

ORACLE OF DELPHI

The Oracle delivered divine prophecies through a priestess at the Sanctuary of Apollo. The priestess practised consciousness-altering rituals, which probably included chewing laurel leaves and poppies and inhaling the vapours rising from a natural chasm where Python had been imprisoned. She communicated the prophecies in a series of inarticulate cries, which priests translated into verse.

See map on pp114–15

Byzantine art in Dafni monastery

8 Dafni

MAP T2 ■ 210 581 1558 ■ Bus 866 or 876 from Metro Agia Marina towards Aspropyrgos (30-minute journey) ■ Open 8:30am–5pm Wed–Sun (winter: to 3:30pm)

The lovely, domed, 11th-century monastic church here, decorated with brilliant mosaics, is one of the greatest treasures of Byzantine art.

9 Mount Parnitha

MAP T2

This beautiful mountain has many walking paths lined with pine and fir forests, though they have reduced since the wildfires of 2007, 2021 and 2023. In spring, its meadows are full of wildflowers. There are two refuges for climbers and a large casino-cum-alpine hotel, reached by cable car from the suburb of Thrakomakedones, the usual starting point for walks.

10 Galaxidi

MAP Q1 ■ Two buses daily (only one on Sat) from Terminal B; www.ktel-fokidas.gr

This resort on the Gulf of Corinth is a great base for visiting Delphi. Located between turquoise waters and green hills, it is peaceful, except on summer weekends, when Athenians throng here. Take the time to explore the museums and 19th-century mansions.

A DRIVING TRIP FROM ATHENS TO DELPHI

DAY ONE

Set out from Athens, breaking up the three-hour drive to Delphi with stops at the monasteries of **Dafni** and **Osios Loukas** *(see p115)*.

Close to Delphi, stay either at the seaside town of **Galaxidi**, if it's summer, or in the mountain village of **Arahova** in winter. If the former, check into the charming **Hotel Ganimede** *(see p149)* and spend the afternoon at the beach; if the latter, consider a family chalet at the **Elatos Resort & Health Club** *(see p148)*. Here, you can take the afternoon to ski (in winter) at the Parnassos Ski Centre, or to explore the many mountain trails.

DAY TWO

The next day, head to the ancient site of **Delphi** bright and early. Wander around the **Temple of Apollo**, considering the strange rituals of the ancient priestesses who delivered the Oracle's pronouncements. Be sure not to miss the **museum** or the nearby **Sanctuary of Athena Pronaia** *(see p118)*.

If you are in a hurry to return to Athens, grab a snack at the taverna **Ta Skalakia** *(p119)* in Delphi. If not, try the feta in filo pastry with honey at **O Bebelis** in Galaxidi, or the sausages and grilled formaella cheese at Arahova's **Karaouli** *(see p119)*.

Sanctuary of Athena Pronaia

Sights in Delphi

1 Sacred Way

This road retraces the route Apollo first followed to Delphi and ends at the temple dedicated to him. The view, of Mount Parnassos looming above and the plunging gorge below, is suitably humbling.

2 Temple of Apollo

This temple contained the *omphalos* (navel-stone), marking the centre of the world, as well as the Oracle. Most ancient authors mention how rulers from all over the world sent envoys with lavish offerings to hear the Oracle's prophecies.

3 Sifnian Treasury

This temple-like marble structure, built by envoys from Sifnos, was the richest and most beautiful of several similar treasuries, all built as offerings to the Oracle. Its statues are now displayed in the museum.

4 Theatre

Built in the 4th century BCE, this is one of the best-preserved theatres of ancient Greece. It offers a sweeping view of the whole site, especially the dramatically varied landscape that makes Delphi sacred.

5 Roman Agora

This marketplace area was lined with stalls selling sacred objects, where visitors could buy offerings to the Oracle.

6 Delphi Museum

2265 082 312 ■ Museum: open summer: 10am–5pm Mon, 8am–8pm Tue–Sun; winter: 8am–3pm daily ■ Site: open 8am–8pm daily (winter & public holidays: to 3pm) ■ Adm

The museum houses the greatest offerings brought to the Oracle from around the world.

Athenian Treasury

7 Athenian Treasury

The Athenians decorated their offering with elegant friezes depicting their hometown heroes Theseus and Herakles. The latter's famous Twelve Labours were performed at the Oracle's behest.

8 Sanctuary of Athena Pronaia

The sanctuary to warrior-goddess Athena was believed to protect the Sanctuary of Apollo from invaders. Though many of the buildings have been destroyed, the enigmatic and round Tholos is the quintessential image of Delphi.

9 Sanctuary of the Earth Goddess

This rock circle around an opening in the earth celebrated the earliest deity associated with the Delphic Oracle: the earth goddess Gaia. The tradition of the Oracle and priestesses continued, under the later deity Apollo.

10 Castalian Spring

Though now mostly dry, this spring was where pilgrims purified themselves before entering the holy site. The elaborate fountain-house built around it is still visible.

Delphi Museum exhibit

Places to Eat

PRICE CATEGORIES

For a three-course meal for one with half a bottle of wine (or equivalent meal), taxes and extra charges.

€ under €40 €€ €40–€60 €€€ over €60

1 Ta Skalakia

MAP Q1 ■ Ilia Sengouni, Delfi ■ 6944 207 532 ■ €

Located on a stepped lane between the two main roads, this friendly place serves grilled local meat as well as more elaborate dishes.

2 Gargadoyas

MAP Q1 ■ Dimou Fragkou 12, Delfi ■ 2265 083 074 ■ €

A favourite among locals and visitors, this place is a carnivore heaven.

3 Kaplanis

MAP R1 ■ Platía Tropeon, Arahova ■ 2267 031 891 ■ €

Flavourful meaty classics served in a room with gilded chandeliers. In spring or fall, try the fried courgette (zucchini) flowers. Year round, sample the excellent house wine.

4 Ab oVo

MAP Q1 ■ Akti Oianthis 87, Galaxidi ■ 693 686 7130 ■ €

Delicious Mediterranean dishes – fish, seafood and pizza – at a friendly restaurant by the port.

5 Karaouli

MAP R1 ■ Arachovas-Eptalofou road, Distomo Arachova Antikira ■ 2267 031 001 ■ Open Sep–Jun: Fri–Sun ■ €

A simple, traditional and delicious taverna. Try the homemade spicy Arahova sausage and stuffed peppers.

6 O Bebelis

MAP Q1 ■ Nikolaou Mama 20–22, Galaxidi ■ 2265 041 677 ■ €

Family-run O Bebelis serves Greek dishes such as caramelized stuffed onions, and pork with peppers in a cosy setting with an open fireplace.

7 Babis

MAP R1 ■ Kalyvia Livadi, Arachova ■ 2267 032 155 ■ Open Oct–Apr: L daily and D Sat & Sun ■ €

Go for a bowl of hot, aromatic *stifado* stew *(see p64)*, as the crackling fire casts a warm glow over everything.

8 Lykos Winery Restaurant

MAP T1 ■ Malakonta, west of Eretria, Évia ■ 222 906 8222 ■ €€

Expect traditional Greek meat and fish dishes and fresh salads, plus excellent wines. Lykos also runs tours and tastings.

Elegant interiors of Taverna Nondas

9 Taverna Nondas

MAP R1 ■ 2 km (1.5 miles) from Livadia ■ 2261 025 422 ■ €

Just outside Livadia, with ample seating both indoors and out, Nondas specializes in roast meats – charcoal-grilled lamb chops, home-made burgers and tender steak – accompanied by colourful salads. Generous portions.

10 Apanemo

MAP T1 ■ Ethnikis Symfiliosis 78, Halkida, Évia ■ 2221 022 614 ■ €

Halkida is well-known for its seafood *mezedopolia* which line the waterfront. Apanemo is perfectly set northeast of the pedestrian bridge. It serves all the seafood standards as well as local specialities such as *petrosolines* (razor clams).

See map on pp114–15

TOP 10 Into the Peloponnese

Statue in a museum in Ancient Corinth

Across the Corinth Canal, west of Athens, lies the Peloponnese, the part of Greece most steeped in myth and history. The Mycenaean kingdoms of Homer's *Iliad* were once believed to be merely legendary, until 19th-century German archaeologist Heinrich Schliemann unearthed their fabulous palaces on the Argive Peninsula. Now these sites compete with those in Athens as the most important in Greece. But, unlike Athens, the landscapes of those legends – the plains, where, according to Homer, great armies assembled, and the fields of Nemea where Herakles wrestled a lion to death – have remained mostly unchanged for millennia, making this one of the most beautiful regions of Greece, as well as the most fascinating.

THE PELOPONNESE

Previous pages A yacht sailing through the Corinth Canal

Ferries sailing in the Corinth Canal

1 Corinth Canal

MAP R3

The isthmus connecting mainland Greece to the Peloponnese frustrated sailors for thousands of years, forcing them to make long, dangerous journeys around the peninsula. Roman emperors Nero and Caligula tried digging a canal, but success came only in 1893, after French engineers had dynamited their way through the rock for 11 years. Boats take about an hour to make the 6-km (4-mile) journey.

2 Mycenae (Mykines)

MAP R3 ■ Open 8am–8pm daily (Apr: to 7pm; winter: to 3pm; shoulder season: hours vary) ■ Adm

Legend and history combine alluringly at Mycenae. Homer wrote of Greece's most powerful king during the Trojan War, Agamemnon, commanding the citadel of "well-built Mycenae, rich in gold." History confirms that there was indeed a Trojan War and a powerful civilization in Mycenae. Heinrich Schliemann uncovered the palace at Mycenae in 1874, much of which accords with Homer's descriptions, including the wealth of gold.

3 Gaia Wines

MAP R3 ■ Koutsi ■ 2746 022 057 ■ 10:30am–4:30pm Wed–Sun; book well in advance in summer ■ www.gaiawines.gr

The Greek wine industry has gained international acclaim by bringing serious cultivation techniques to its sun-drenched soils and indigenous grapes. Gaia is one of the best vineyards, producing deep velvety wines from Nemea's Agiogiorgitiko red and some white grapes.

4 Acrocorinth (Akrokorinthos)

MAP R3 ■ 2741 031 207, 2741 031 266 ■ Open 8:30am–3:30pm daily

This towering rock outside Corinth was the strongest natural fortification in ancient Greece. In Archaic times it was crowned by a famous temple to Aphrodite. The structures you see today are mostly medieval Ottoman, often having been built over much older buildings. Stunning views reward the effort to hike to the top.

The rock of Acrocorinth

Colourful side street, Nafplio

5 Nafplio

MAP R3

Small, seaside Nafplio is one of Greece's most beautiful towns. For years the Ottomans and Venetians fought for the city, leaving behind two hilltop Venetian fortresses and several mosques. The Greeks seized Nafplio early in the independence war and made it their first capital in 1829, before Athens took that mantle.

6 Ancient Corinth

MAP R3 ■ 274 103 1207 ■ Open summer: 8am–8pm daily (Apr: to 7pm); winter: 8:30am–3:30pm daily; shoulder season hours vary, call ahead ■ Adm

Corinth's location, between the Peloponnese and mainland Greece, made it a powerful trading centre since the Mycenaean times. Material wealth came with the image of wild and licentious lifestyles, including polygamy and orgiastic cults, which St Paul addressed with great concern in the Bible. An earthquake in 1928 and a fire in 1933 destroyed the city. Today Corinth's appeal resides in the ruins of its ancient glories, especially the 6th-century BCE Temple of Apollo, and the superb on site museum.

7 Argos

MAP R3 ■ Ancient theatre: Open 8:30am–3:30pm daily ■ Adm

Believed to be the longest continually inhabited town in Greece, this modern town sits on top of the ancient one. The 4th-century BCE theatre, overlooking the ancient city and visible from the Argolic Gulf, was one of the largest of ancient Greece, seating close to 20,000 spectators. If you have a car, drive up the Aspis hill, to the medieval castle of Larissa overlooking the plain immortalized by Homer.

THE LABOURS OF HERAKLES

Herakles was the son of Zeus and the mortal Alkmene. Hera, enraged at her husband Zeus's infidelity, drove Herakles mad, causing him to kill his family. In penance, he was required to perform 12 feats of heroism, out of which six of them around the Peloponnese. He was cleansed of his sin and glorified for his feats, which, ironically, are attributed to the jealous goddess: his name means "glory of Hera".

The Temple of Apollo in Ancient Corinth, with Acrocorinth in background

8 Epidauros

MAP S3 ■ Open 8am–8pm daily (Apr: to 7pm; winter: to 5pm; shoulder season hours vary) ■ Adm

The 4th-century BCE Theatre of Epidauros is one of the best sites in Greece, marvellously preserved and with astounding acoustics *(see p72)*. Outside the theatre is the restored Asklepion, an ancient sanctuary devoted to Asklepios, the god of health.

Theatre of Epidauros

9 Nemea

MAP R3 ■ Open summer: 8am–8pm daily (Apr: to 7pm); winter: 8:30am–3pm Wed–Mon; shoulder season hours vary ■ Adm

This was the site of the first labour of Herakles: the slaying of the Nemean lion. The lion's skin was impenetrable, so Herakles strangled the beast, skinned it with its own claws and kept its pelt as a coat of armour. This is one of several legends connected with the Nemean Games (part of the Panhellenic Games). The highlight of Nemea is the temple of Zeus, with nine columns and two architraves that have been reconstructed.

10 Tiryns

MAP R3 ■ Open 8:30am–3:30pm daily ■ Adm

One of the most important cities of the Mycenaean civilization, Tiryns is known for its massive limestone fortifications; later Greeks even believed they could have been built by the giant Kyklopes. Although not as grand as Mycenae, Tiryns has intriguing details on its walls.

OVERNIGHT IN NAFPLIO

DAYTIME

Visit **Nafplio** on a summer weekend, buying tickets for a performance at Epidauros before setting off *(see p43)*.

Take a morning bus from Athens' Terminal A, having also booked a hotel in advance. The nicest place to stay is Nafplia Palace; Hotel Byron is more affordable but still good.

Spend the day exploring Nafplio's Old City. Take some drinks and a snack, and carry them up to the **Venetian fortress**, which affords glorious views of Nafplio and the Gulf of Argos. If you're feeling fit, climb the 999 steps to the top; otherwise, take a taxi.

Below the fortress, cool off at the small public beach. For more privacy, head down the walkway and go diving from the rocks.

NIGHTTIME

Dine at Aiolos Tavern *(see p127)*, returning to the bus station before 7:30pm, when buses depart for **Epidauros**. Even if the performance is in Greek, the powerful acting and magical setting will captivate. Programmes summarize the plot and there are subtitles in English. Take the bus back to Nafplio and the hotel.

The following morning, check out, but leave your luggage at the hotel. Take an early bus to **Mycenae** *(see p123)*, whose tragic former inhabitants may well have been the subject of the previous night's play. Marvel at this legendary prehistoric city for a few hours, then go back to Nafplio and hop on a bus back to Athens.

See map on p122

The Best of the Rest

1 Isthmia

MAP R3 ■ 2741 037 244 ■ 8:30am–3:30pm Wed–Mon ■ Adm

Much of the ancient site of Isthmia has been destroyed, but a number of mosaics of marine creatures remain. Here visitors can enjoy the vibrant 4th-century CE opus sectile panels portraying harbour scenes, bird-life and sea creatures.

2 Loutraki

MAP R2 ■ Hydrotherapeutic Thermal Spa: Georgiou Lekka 24 ■ www.loutrakispa.gr

A popular weekend destination, Loutraki is known for its spring waters and its Hydrotherapeutic Thermal Spa. This pleasant town on the Gulf of Corinth also has a fine beach.

3 Heraion of Perahora

MAP R2

Though little remains here other than a Temple of Hera and a stoa, this is still an idyllic place to swim, with the wonderful Melangavi lighthouse, and crystal-clear waters. Snorkellers can see ancient ruins underwater.

Beach shore and sanctuary at Perahora

4 Kekhries

MAP R3

The site where Theseus defeated Sinis, the bandit who used whole pine trees to sling-shot victims across the water. Today the seaside town makes a nice stop on the drive to Epidauros.

5 Loutra Oreas Elenis

MAP R3

A perfect lunch stop en route from Athens to Epidauros, this seaside village offers swimming and is dotted with choice tavernas. According to legend, Helen of Troy once bathed in the small, warm spring here.

6 Heraion of Argos

MAP R3 ■ N of Nafplio ■ Open 8:30am–3:30pm daily

This sanctuary to goddess Hera, built between the 8th and 4th centuries BCE, occupies three raised terraces, with great views over the Argive plain.

7 Skouras Wines

MAP R3 ■ On Argos–Nemea road, nr Synora village ■ Opening hours vary, check website (book in advance) ■ www.skouras.gr

Skouras is known for its range of quality white, red and rosé wines. Agiorgitiko is a speciality.

8 Lerna

MAP R4 ■ Open 8:30am–3:30pm daily ■ Adm

One of the oldest archaeological sites in Greece, with remains dating back to 2500 BCE.

9 Agia Moni

MAP R3 ■ Nr Nafplio

This 12th-century Byzantine convent and garden is worth a short stop when visiting Nafplio.

10 Asine

MAP R4

This fortified Bronze Age settlement is set near a beach. Nobel Laureate George Seferis paid homage to this place in his poem *The King of Asine*.

Places to Eat

1 Omorfo Tavernaki

MAP R3 ■ Epameinonda Kotsonopoulos 1, Nafplio ■ 2752 025 944 ■ €

With a romantic interior, this taverna offers traditional Greek dishes. It gets crowded during the Epidauros festival, so book in advance.

2 Stavlos Thrakotaverna

MAP R3 ■ Profiti Ilia 12, Nafplio ■ 2752 306 702 ■ €

Sample lamb dishes and *kokoretsi* (offal on a spit) at this taverna. Meat-lovers would enjoy feasting here.

Delicious *kokoretsi* with potato fries

3 Taverna Akrogiali

MAP R4 ■ Aktis 10, Tolo ■ 275 205 9789 ■ €

This beach-side taverna offers a wide range of delicious fish, seafood and meat dishes, as well as meze and vegetarian options.

4 Aiolos Tavern

MAP R3 ■ Vasilissis Olgas 30, Nafplio ■ 2752 026 828 ■ €

Set in the heart of Nafplio, this cheerful family-run taverna offers traditional fare, from slow-cooked beans and grilled meats to cabbage rolls.

5 To Pefko

MAP R3 ■ Loutra Oreas Elenis ■ 2741 033 801 ■ €

With outdoor seating, this restaurant offers tasty squid and sand smelt, as well as plenty of vegetarian options, paired with rosé wine. Take a quick dip until your order arrives.

PRICE CATEGORIES

For a three-course meal for one with half a bottle of wine (or equivalent meal), taxes and extra charges.

€ under €40 **€€** €40–€60 **€€€** over €60

6 Psalidas

MAP R3 ■ Lefkakia, 7 km (4 miles) E of Nafplio ■ 2752 061 814 ■ €

In the sleepy village of Lefkakia, Psalidas serves traditional home cooking in a pretty garden. Expect meaty stews, seasonal vegetables such as artichokes in spring and peppers in summer, and excellent local red wine. Book ahead on weekends.

7 Maria's Restaurant

MAP R4 ■ Bouboulinas 48, Tolo ■ 2752 059 198 ■ €

Above the bay of Tolo, enjoy spectacular views and delicious dishes prepared with Mediterranean finesse and served with style in a room open to the sky. Try the wonderful spaghetti with fresh clams.

8 Kalogerikon

MAP R3 ■ Nik. Pitidi, Panagia ■ 2753 042 090 ■ €

Housed in a stone-built coastal resort, this restaurant has an inviting garden and orange grove. Enjoy seasonal meat dishes and *moussakas* with wine.

9 Rigani

MAP R2 ■ Papanikolaou 5, Loutraki ■ 2744 066 744 ■ €

With its innovative approach to traditional recipes, Rigani offers high-quality taverna food. Enjoy it in the cool garden, framed and shaded by trees and vineyards.

10 Mouria Restaurant - Gikas Holidays Club

MAP S3 ■ Palea Epidavros, Argolida ■ 2753 041 218 ■ €

The food here is rooted firmly in the Greek tradition: fresh locally caught fish, fine grilled meats and delicious home-made desserts.

See map on p122

TOP 10 Around the Attica Coast

Throughout antiquity, the ancients built marble temples to their gods on Attica's verdant, pine-covered slopes. This is a land where the legendary Theseus once roamed, freeing Attica from a scourge of monsters. Crowning the peninsula, at southernmost Cape Sounio, was the stunning Temple of Poseidon, sparkling like a beacon over the Aegean. Looking at Attica today, it is clear to see that parts of the coast have fallen victim to overdevelopment, but its jewels remain in the peacefully crumbling temples among the trees, in the best of the region's sandy beaches and in the ultra-luxurious summer clubs, which stretch down the coast as far as Varkiza.

Temple of Artemis, Brauron

THE ATTICA COAST

The picturesque thermal Lake Vouliagmeni, offering year-round bathing

1 Lake Vouliagmeni

MAP T3 ■ Bus 122 from Argyroupoli metro ■ Open: 8am–8pm (winter: to 5pm); book in advance ■ Adm ■ www.limnivouliagmenis.gr

Bathers come year-round to take the warm, therapeutic waters of Lake Vouliagmeni, a large thermal spring that maintains a steady temperature of 22–25°C (72–77°F). The source of the clear, half-fresh, half-salt waters is still unknown, but devotees say there's no doubt about their healing properties. It's a great place to swim, especially on cold winter mornings, flanked by a high rock face on one side and trees on the other.

2 Vouliagmeni

MAP T3 ■ Bus 117/122 from Argyroupoli metro

A sprawling seaside resort suburb south of Athens, Vouliagmeni is fringed with luxury hotels, yacht clubs and pricey pay-per-visit beaches. But the biggest draw for Athenians and visitors are the super-glam beachside clubs, the centre of nightlife in summer. All are re-created in luscious over-the-top decor each year.

3 Temple of Artemis, Brauron

MAP T3 ■ Markopoulo, Mesogia ■ 2299 027 020 ■ Open 8:30am–3:30pm Wed–Mon ■ Adm

This temple to Artemis, goddess of the hunt and childbirth, was once the most sacred in Attica. Its highlight was the Arkteia festival, where young girls dressed as cubs performed the "bear dance" in honour of the goddess's favourite animal. In some versions of the myth of Iphigenia, the goddess saved her from sacrifice and brought her here, where she became a high priestess. Her tomb is the oldest cult shrine on the site. The tranquil site is complete with a colonnade and a sacred spring. It also offers an excellent museum that was refurbished in 2009.

Shopping in Glyfada

4 Glyfada

MAP T3 ■ Bus 122 or 171 from Argyroupoli metro, or tram from Syntagma

Glyfada is the beginning of a stretch of glamourous seaside districts extending towards Cape Sounion – the Athens Riviera – a prime destination for beach clubs, cafés and boutiques.

Ruins at the Amphiario Sanctuary

5 Amphiario Sanctuary

MAP T2 ■ 2295 062 144 ■ Open 8:30am–3:30pm daily ■ Adm

Dedicated in the late 5th century BCE, this shrine was an oracle and a health resort. It honoured Amphiaraos, King of Argos, tricked into fighting against Thebes, even though he foresaw that he would be killed. Zeus arranged for the earth to swallow him on the battlefield, and be reincarnated as a demi-god. There is a small theatre complete with stage and a stoa.

6 Temple of Poseidon

MAP T3 ■ 2292 039 363 ■ KTEL bus from Nomismatokopeio metro ■ Open 9:30am–sunset daily ■ Adm

The 5th-century BCE temple is one of the few ever built to Poseidon.

THE LOCAL HERO

Theseus is linked with Attica through a mix of mythology and enticing traces of historical evidence that suggest that a King Theseus may have actually existed. This king managed to unite the region's splinter states, while the reputation of Theseus the hero rests on tales of his slaying villains and monsters, including most famously the minotaur.

After watching the sunset from the white marble pillars of this ancient site on the peak of Cape Sounio, you may share the sentiments of the poet Byron. He asked the gods simply to "Place me on Sunium's marbled steep, Where nothing save the waves and I, May hear our mutual murmurs sweep, There, swanlike, let me sing and die." *(See also p53.)*

7 Marathon (Marathonas)

MAP T2 ■ Marathon tomb: 2294 055 462 ■ Museum: 2294 055 155 ■ Open 8:30am–3:30pm Wed–Mon (for both all year round) ■ KTEL bus from Nomismatokopeio metro ■ Adm (for both)

In 490 BCE, the Marathon plain was the site of one of history's most important battles. There, an army of 10,000 Greeks defeated 25,000 Persians, preserving the newly founded first democracy. A tomb to the 192 Greek soldiers who fell (in comparison to 6,000 Persians) still stands here. After the victory, Pheidippides ran the 42 km (26 miles) to Athens to announce the outcome, then collapsed dead on the spot. A museum displays finds from the area.

Temple of Poseidon on Cape Sounio

8 Skhinias

MAP T2 ■ KTEL bus from Nomismatokopeio metro

Many consider Skhinias the most beautiful beach area in Attica, its white-sand coast hugged by dark pine forests. An giant rowing course was constructed on the wetlands for the 2004 Olympics, despite this being an environmentally protected area. Several rustic, illegal tavernas at the beach have been demolished. However, visitors can lunch at the nearby Marathonas beach.

9 Ramnous (Ramnounda)

MAP T2 ■ Open 8:30am–3:30pm Wed–Mon ■ Adm

The 5th-century ruins of these temples to Nemesis (goddess of divine retribution) and Themis (goddess justice and law) are among Greece's most unspoiled sites. There is an ancient fortress situated just adjacent, which defended the important harbour.

Temple ruins at Ramnous

10 Rafina

MAP T2 ■ KTEL bus from Nomismatokopeio metro

If you go to the islands of Andros or Évia, you'll spend time in Rafina, Attica's third port along with Piraeus and Lavrio. It's smaller and cleaner than chaotic Piraeus, but still bustling, filled with quayside seafood tavernas as well as the traffic of embarking and disembarking ferries. The environs of Rafina were devastated by a firestorm in July 2018 but growth is now slowly returning to the region.

A TOUR OF ATTICA

MORNING

Start early with a drive out of Athens to **Marathonas**. Survey the plain where the Greeks won history's greatest military victory, and pay homage at the warriors' tomb. Then head to the ruins of **Ramnous**, focusing more on the scenery than the site's original purpose: praying for revenge.

Drive south down the coast, to the **Temple of Artemis** at **Brauron** and its museum *(see p129)*, which closes at 3pm. Then have lunch at **To Korali** *(Vravrona Beach 367; 2294 045 044; open all day from noon)*

AFTERNOON

Head to one of Greece's most splendid sights: the **Temple of Poseidon** at Sounio. If it's still daylight, go to one of the two nearby beaches. The one to the east of the temple access lane requires an athletic scramble down but offers scenic seclusion; the hotel beach to the northwest is more accessible but covered with sun loungers. An hour before sunset, wander up to the temple, and watch as the marble columns turn to pink and gold.

Returning to the coastal drive to Athens, consider two dinner options. The nearby taverna **Syrtaki**, back towards Lavrio, or, closer to the city, the elegant **Pelagos** *(see p133)* in the Four Seasons Astir Palace, where you can end your day with a romantic view of the Aegean Sea below a starlit sky.

See map on p128

Nearby Islands

1 Salamina (Salamis)
MAP S3

Ancient Salamis had a rich history. Playwright Euripides was born here, and in 480 BCE, the Greeks famously beat Xerxes off the shore. Visit the Faneromeni convent for its frescoes as well as the clean south coast beaches.

2 Spetses
MAP S4

Popular with British tourists, Spetses offers pine forests, good beaches and a charming harbour town. Automobiles are restricted in town, but allowed along the island ring road.

3 Angistri
MAP S3

This tiny hispter islet off Egina has several beaches, clear beautiful water, a handful of small hotels and tavernas, and not much else.

4 Poros
MAP S4

Volcanic Poros comprises two joined islands, Sferia and Kalavria. The town of Sferia is worth a visit, and Kalavria has pine trees, beaches as well as the Zoödohou Pigis monastery.

5 Hydra (Ydra)
MAP S4

Lovely Hydra town, its marble-paved, car-free lanes winding among the old mansions around the busy harbour, is one of Greece's most beautiful spots. Its popularity as a celebrity getaway hasn't dented its charm.

Seafront at Hydra

6 Egina
MAP S3

An easy and rewarding day trip, only 45 minutes from Athens, with an atmospheric town, famously tasty pistachios, the Temple of Aphaia, and the ghost village of Paleohora, with several frescoed chapels.

Temple of Aphaia at Egina

7 Kea (Tzia)
MAP U3

Although only an hour by ferry from Lavrio, Kea is peaceful and away from the port, and its interior is covered by oak trees. Don't miss the Archaic Lion of Kea, carved into a hillside.

8 Andros
MAP V3

A favourite of Greece's wealthy, golden-beached Andros is exclusive and hiker-friendly. The Goulandris Museum of Contemporary Art, Greece's first contemporary art museum, holds interesting exhibits every summer.

9 Kythnos
MAP U4

It might not be as picturesque as the other Cyclades but Kythnos has thermal springs at Loutra and great beaches.

10 Évia
MAP S1–U2

Only the southern part of Évia is easily visited from Athens. The main attractions here are the Neo-Classical town of Karystos, nearby beaches and the hiking trails on Mount Ohi.

Places to Eat

PRICE CATEGORIES

For a three-course meal for one with half a bottle of wine (or equivalent meal), taxes and extra charges.

€ under €40 €€ €40–€60 €€€ over €60

1 Christina, Hydra

MAP S4 ■ 70 m (230 ft) inland from the Kamini port ■ 2298 053 516 ■ €

This garden and sea-to-table family-run taverna, under the shade in Kamini, is a local favourite.

2 O Psaras

MAP T2 ■ Leoforos Poseidonos 3, Marathonas Beach ■ 2294 055 237 ■ €

Enjoy octopus, barbecued fresh fish and a Greek salad under canvas sunshades on a wooden deck on Marathon's sandy beach. Start with their exceptional *mezedes*.

3 Parnasssos

MAP T2 ■ Metohi hamlet, Angistri islet ■ 2297 091 339 ■ €

Apart from standard grills and starters, this inland spot above the port serves its own cheese, a few daily *magirefta* and decent *hyma* wine.

4 Platanos

MAP T3 ■ Platia Agiou Georgiou, Poros ■ 2298 026 661 ■ €

Set inland under a *platanos* (plane tree), this taverna serves meat grills as well as seafood. It also offers plenty of vegetarian options.

5 Patralis, Spetses

MAP S4 ■ Kounopitsa waterfront ■ 2298 075 380 ■ €

Specializing in seafood, this taverna offers fish in Spetsiota sauce and *astakomakaronada* (noodles with lobster flakes). Great terrace views.

6 Syrtaki, nr Sounio

MAP T3 ■ 2 km (1 mile) N of Poseidon Temple, towards, Lavrio ■ 2292 039 125 ■ €€

The most popular taverna around Sounio. Eat seafood at the shaded three-storey seating area, which offers great views of the sea.

7 O Paparounas, Kea

MAP U3 ■ Ioulida ■ 2288 022 583 ■ €

O Paparounas is known for its seafood. The pistachio-crusted feta is great too.

8 Endochora, Andros

MAP V3 ■ G. Embirikou, Andros Town ■ 2282 023 207 ■ €

In Andros' car-free Old Town, Endochora serves contemporary Mediterranean fare in a white-washed shabby-chic interior. Try a variety of cheese with candied grapes, grilled salmon with wild rice, and their signature cucumber salad with poppy seeds and chilli sauce.

Traditional Greek salad with feta cheese

9 Deka, Egina

MAP S3 ■ Perdika waterfront ■ 2297 061 231 ■ €

Around since 1943, this is the oldest and most reliable taverna at the harbour. The menu includes exceptional and well-priced seafood.

10 Pelagos, Vouliagmeni

MAP T3 ■ Apollonos 40 ■ 210 890 1192 ■ €€€

Located in the upmarket Four Seasons Astir Palace Hotel, the Michelin-starred Pelagos is popular for its sea-view terrace and tasting menus featuring Mediterranean cuisine with classic French influences. Enjoy the flavours of the carefully sourced artisanal island ingredients.

See map on p128

Streetsmart

Evzones at the Changing of the Guard

Getting Around

Arriving by Air

Athens International Airport (Eleftherios Venizelos) lies 27 km (16.5 miles) southeast of the city centre, to which it is connected by various means of public transport. The metro (line 3, blue) runs half hourly from the airport to Syntagma and Monastiraki, in the city centre but services stop just before midnight. In addition, there are four 24-hour bus services: the X95 runs to Syntagma; the X96 to Piraeus port; the X93 to the KTEL Kifissos bus station; and the X97 to Elliniko metro station (line 2, red). Look up timetables on the **Athens Transport** website. Taxis are also readily available; the trip to the city centre takes about 40 minutes in light traffic and operates on a fixed tariff.

Aegean Airlines, the largest Greek airline, flies into Athens from most European capitals, including London, Edinburgh, Dublin, Paris, Rome, Berlin and Madrid, as well as from Russia and the Middle East. **British Airways, Ryanair**, Jet2 and easyJet fly in from the UK, while **Delta** flies direct from New York (JFK) in the US, and **Air Canada** and **Air Transat** fly direct from several points in Canada.

Arriving by Sea

Athens is served by the port of Piraeus, among Europe's largest and busiest passenger ports. There are frequent ferry services to and from the Argo-Saronic islands, Crete, the Cyclades, the Northeast Aegean and the Dodecanese, transporting both locals and visitors alike. Many cruise ships sailing around the eastern Mediterranean also dock at Piraeus. To travel into the city centre, you can catch the metro from Piraeus station at the harbour. There are plenty of taxis available, although in high season you may have to wait in line.

The smaller port of Rafína, to the east of the city, sees ferry departures for Evia and islands in the Cyclades. Southeast of Athens, Lávrio offers services to the Cyclades and to the Northeast Aegean.

For ferry timetables and booking, see the **Greek Ferries**, **GTP** or **Ferryhopper** websites, which cover every main company that has operations from the islands.

Train Travel

Greece's railway infrastructure is under the umbrella of Ferrovie dello Stato Italiane and is operated by **Hellenic Train**. Safety and hygiene measures, ticket information, transport maps and timetables can be found on the Hellenic Train website.

Athens forms the hub of the system. Four daily departures from Athens' main railway station, Stathmos Larisis, connect the capital with Thessaloníki. The journey takes approximately five hours. From Thessaloníki, there are lines travelling west to Flórina and east to Drama.

A new standard-gauge line is being built linking Piraeus with Pátra, the only passenger service on the Peloponnese. At the moment, there's a train service to Kiato. Passengers heading for Pátra need to change to a Hellenic Train bus to reach their final destination. Check the Hellenic Train website for the latest updates.

Long-Distance Bus Travel

Greece has an excellent bus network, not just between cities but in rural areas too. It is run by **KTEL** (Koinó Tameío Eispráxeon Leoforeíon), a syndicate of many regional private companies. Every community in the country is provided with services of some sort, though the frequency of these varies greatly.

Long-distance coaches from all over Greece run to Athens, ending their journeys at either **KTEL Kifissos** (Bus Terminal A) or **KTEL Liosion** (Bus Terminal B), both northwest of the city centre. (Each terminal serves a different set of destinations.) Coaches serving Attiki as well as Thessaloniki leave from the **KTEL Attikis** bus station near the Nosmimatokopeio metro station and other locations, depending on the route. Ticket sales are computerized for all major routes, with reserved seating on modern coaches (for Attikis, tickets are bought with cash on board). It is wise to buy your ticket in advance, since seats often sell out and coaches tend to leave early. You may need extra time to exchange your online ticket for a paper one before departure.

Public Transport

Athens has a three-line metro system, which shares tickets with the small tramway network and extensive bus routes. The metro has three lines: Line 1 (green line) runs north to south with several central stops, and offers visitors the fastest way of reaching Piraeus. Line 2 (red line) runs from northwest Athens to the southeast. At Sýntagma it intersects with Line 3 (blue line), which runs from Piraeus through western Athens to Doukíssis Plakentías in the northeast, with some trains continuing on to Athens International Airport. Tickets must be validated before boarding the train – use the machines found at the entrances to all platforms.

Athens is served by an extensive bus network, covering over 300 routes. Journeys are inexpensive but can be slow and crowded, especially in the city centre and during rush hours. Timetables and informative route maps are available from **OASA**, the Athens Urban Transport Organization.

Athens also has a good network of trolleybuses that run on electricity on over 20 routes, connecting many of the main sights. Tickets can be bought at machines or windows at metro stations; contactless debit cards can be used, too, but make sure to check beforehand that there's no surcharge from your bank.

The rudimentary tram system in Athens connects the city centre and the coast, and has the same ticketing system.

Tickets and Travel Cards

Tickets for public transport come in the form of reusable **ATH.ENA** cards, of which there are three types available: paper, an anonymous plastic card and a personalized plastic card. All are rechargeable and can be purchased and topped up at ticket booths and machines in any metro or tram station; very few *periptera* (streetcorner kiosks) will stock them. You can also tap in with a contactless debit card.

Tickets are integrated to cover bus, trolleybus, tram and metro (but not routes to the airport). One ticket costs €1.20 and is valid for 90 minutes from the moment you stamp it at the beginning of your first journey; you can load many journeys onto a single card, and the price drops the more you add – eg €2.30 for two trips, €6.50 for five trips at any time. A day ticket costs €4.10 and a five-day ticket €8.20. For the airport, a single express bus ticket is €6 and a regular metro ticket is €9 (there are discounts for two or more passengers). A tourist ticket is available for €20 and includes a round trip to the airport, metro, tram and bus for three days. There are reductions on some fares for those over 65, children and students.

DIRECTORY

ARRIVING BY AIR

Aegean Airlines
W en.aegeanair.com

Air Canada
W aircanada.com

Air Transat
W airtransat.com

Athens International Airport
W aia.gr

Athens Transport
W athenstransport.com

British Airways
W britishairways.com

Delta
W delta.com

Ryanair
W ryanair.com

ARRIVING BY SEA

Ferryhopper
W ferryhopper.com

Greek Ferries
W greekferries.gr

GTP
W gtp.gr

TRAIN TRAVEL

Hellenic Train
W hellenictrain.gr

LONG-DISTANCE BUS TRAVEL

KTEL
W ktelbus.com

KTEL Attikis
Patission 68
T 210 880 8000

KTEL Kifissos
Leoforos Kifisou 100
T 210 512 4910

KTEL Liosion
Liosion 260
T 210 831 1434

PUBLIC TRANSPORT

ATH.ENA
W athenacard.gr

OASA
W oasa.gr

Guided Bus Tours

Several companies, including **Athens Hop-On Hop-Off**, offer open-top double-decker buses on a hop-on-hop-off circular tour, starting from Syntagma Square and taking in the city's main attractions, including the Acropolis, the Temple of Olympian Zeus, the Acropolis Museum, the Benaki Museum of Greek Culture and the National Archaeological Museum. A few companies also offer other routes. Buses run daily and offer an audio guide in several languages. Tickets are usually available for 24, 48 or 72 hours.

Taxis

Yellow taxis can be seen cruising the streets of Athens at most times of the day or night. Getting one to stop, however, can be a difficult task, especially between 2pm and 3pm, when drivers usually change shifts. To hail a taxi, stand on the edge of the pavement and shout out your destination to any cab that slows down. You can also find taxi ranks dotted around the city, especially near major squares.

Athenian taxis are generally cheap compared to other European cities; depending on traffic, you should not pay more than €5 to travel to any destination within the downtown area, and about €15 from the centre to Piraeus. Higher tariffs come into effect between midnight and 5am and for journeys that exceed certain distances from the city centre. There are also surcharges for extra luggage weighing more than 10 kg (22 lbs), and for journeys from the ferry or railway terminals. Fares increase during holiday periods, such as Christmas and Easter.

Taxi companies can also be booked online or over the phone. In Athens, the Uber service using private cars is currently suspended, though you can use the **UberTAXI** service to book a taxi and pay through the Uber app.

Driving to Athens

Major roads connecting Greece to its neighbours run to Thessaloníki: the E90 from Turkey, the E79 from Bulgaria and the E75 from North Macedonia. All of these routes merge west of Thessaloníki as the E75/A1 on towards Athens (502 km/312 miles). To the west, Patras is connected to Athens (210 km/130.5 miles) by the A8. Drivers must pay at often closely spaced toll stations.

Car Rental

The minimum age for car rental is 21 years, although some companies require drivers to be over 25. In low season, rental cars can generally be arranged on the spot, but in summer it is advisable to reserve one online in advance on a third-party website, such as **Auto Europe**, or directly with a local agency. All the major international chains have local affiliates in Athens, including **Hertz**, **Avis**, **Budget**, **Enterprise** and **Sixt**. Take out a policy insuring you for the collision damage waiver excess beforehand.

Licences

Driving licences issued by any of the European Union member states are valid in Greece (and throughout the EU). If visiting from outside the EU, you will need to apply in advance for an International Driving Permit. Check with your local automobile association before you travel.

Driving in Athens

Driving in Athens can be a nerve-racking experience and is best avoided, especially if you are not accustomed to Greek road habits. Many streets in the centre are pedestrianized, and there are also plenty of one-way streets, so you need to plan your route carefully. Finding a parking space can be very difficult, too. Contrary to appearances, parking in front of a no-parking sign or on a single yellow line is illegal. There are pay-and-display machines for legal on-street parking, as well as underground car parks and unofficial parking lots, although these often tend to fill up quickly.

In an attempt to reduce high air pollution levels, Athens enforces a strict "odd-even" driving system. Cars that have an odd number at the end of their licence plates can enter the central grid *(daktýlios)* only on dates with an odd number, while cars ending in an even number are allowed into it only on even-numbered dates. To avoid being unable to access the *daktýlios*, some people have two cars – with odd and even plates. The "odd–even" rule does not apply to foreign cars, although it is still advisable to avoid taking your car into the city centre if possible.

Driving in the rest of the country is a less fraught experience, though you may wish to avoid bigger cities like Thessaloníki and Pátra. Major motorways are usually in good condition, but be prepared for potholes and other hazards if you go into more rural areas.

Rules of the Road

The blood alcohol limit is 0.5 g per litre, and driving under the influence will result in fines, possible loss of licence and prosecution. Seatbelts must be worn in front seats, with a €350 fine and up to 20 days' loss of licence for noncompliance. Children aged 12 or under must sit in the back seat and under-threes must ride in approved child seats (rental agencies will supply these). Fines for minor infractions must be paid within ten days to avoid court proceedings.

It's an offence to drive away from an accident involving another car – or to move the vehicles from the positions at which they came to rest – before the arrival of the police, who will breathalyze all drivers and write an accident report. This will be required by your car-hire company and also your insurer, even if you are driving your own vehicle.

Cycling

For years, the idea of riding a bicycle in Athens sounded absurd, but since the onset of the economic crisis, more and more locals have bought bikes and started cycling around the city. However, there are no official bike lanes (although cyclists are now allowed to ride in the bus lanes) and car drivers still have a low tolerance, so take care while riding.

In line with the increase in popularity of cycling, several companies now offer bicycle tours of the city. These include **Athens by Bike**, which provides a guided tour around the main historic sites, and **Trekking Hellas**, which offers a variety of e-bike tours within the city, as well as a day-trip to go mountain biking on Mount Parnitha, on Athens' northern outskirts.

Walking

Athens' city centre is a joy to walk around, and all the main sites can be reached on foot from Syntagma. There is a slowly increasing number of pedestrian-only streets – pick your route carefully and you can avoid traffic altogether. The hilltops of the Acropolis and Lykavittos are visible from many areas of the city and can serve as useful orientation points.

There are numerous walking tours available, often themed around specific aspects of the city's history and culture. **Alternative Athens** offers amusing and informative tours giving an insight into the local lifestyle, covering everything from street art to mythology. Canada-based **Tours by Locals** can organize local freelance guides offering specialist private tours. **Discover Greek Culture** and **Athens Insiders** are great for food, history and culture lovers.

DIRECTORY

GUIDED BUS TOURS

Athens Hop-On Hop-Off
W city-sightseeing.com

TAXIS

UberTAXI
W uber.com

CAR RENTAL

Auto Europe
W autoeurope.co.uk

Avis
W avis.co.uk

Budget
W budget.co.uk

Enterprise
W enterprise.co.uk

Hertz
W hertz.co.uk

Sixt
W sixt.co.uk

CYCLING

Athens by Bike
W athensbybike.gr

Trekking Hellas
W trekking.gr

WALKING

Alternative Athens
W alternativeathens.com

Athens Insiders
W athensinsiders.com

Athens Open Tour
W athensopentour.com

Discover Greek Culture
W discovergreekculture.com

Tours by Locals
W toursbylocals.com

Practical Information

Passports and Visas

For entry requirements, including visas, consult your nearest Greek embassy or check the **Greek Ministry of Foreign Affairs** website. Citizens of the UK, US, Canada, Australia and New Zealand do not need a visa for stays of up to three months, but in future must apply in advance for the European Travel Information and Authorization System **(ETIAS)**. Visitors from other countries may also require an ETIAS, so check before travelling. EU nationals do not need a visa or an ETIAS.

Government Advice

It is important to seek both your and the Greek government advice before travelling. The UK Foreign, Commonwealth & Development Office **(FCDO)**, the **US Department of State**, the **Australian Department of Foreign Affairs and Trade** and the Greek Ministry of Foreign Affairs offer the latest information on security, health and local regulations.

Customs Information

You can find information on the laws relating to goods and currency taken in or out of Greece on the **Greek Ministry of Tourism** website. EU citizens are no longer subjected to export limits on alcohol, tobacco and perfume for personal use. Import limits for EU citizens are: 800 cigarettes, 400 cigarillos, 200 cigars, 1 kg of smoking tobacco, 10 litres of spirits over 22 per cent, 20 litres of alcoholic beverages under 22 per cent, 90 litres of wine (of which only 60 can be sparkling) and 110 litres of beer.

Visitors aged over 17 from non-EU countries can carry the following items in their personal luggage: 1 litre of spirits, 4 litres of still wine and 16 litres of beer. There are strict limits on the import and export of antiquities, archaeological artifacts, firearms and weapons.

Insurance

We recommend taking out a comprehensive insurance policy covering theft, loss of belongings, medical care, cancellations and delays, and to read the small print carefully. Visitors are eligible for emergency medical care in Greece, provided they have a valid European Health Insurance Card (EHIC) or UK Global Health Insurance Card (**GHIC**). Comprehensive travel insurance covering private clinics is highly recommended, particularly for those without an EHIC or GHIC.

Health

Emergency medical care is free or the same cost as for residents of Greece for visitors with an EHIC or GHIC at state-run clinics or hospitals, provided you enter via the casualty ward. If you have an EHIC or GHIC, be sure to present this as soon as possible. For other visitors payment of medical expenses is the patient's responsibility. Organizing comprehensive medical insurance before your trip is essential, as private doctors or clinics within Greece are expensive.

Seek medicinal supplies and advice for minor ailments from pharmacies *(farmakeio)*, which are indicated by a green cross. When they are shut, there will be a sign on the door directing you to the nearest 24-hour service. Visit the **Vrisko** or **Doctor Anytime** websites for more information on accessible medical services in Athens.

Smoking, Alcohol and Drugs

Since 2010, it has been illegal in Greece to smoke in enclosed public spaces including in restaurants, bars and cafés. However, locals often ignore this law. Smoking in outdoor areas such as café terraces is permitted.

Greek police does not tolerate rowdy behaviour, especially when fuelled by excessive alcohol consumption; heavy fines or even prison sentences may be imposed on people who behave indecently. Possession of narcotics is prohibited and could result in a prison sentence.

ID

Both locals and foreign visitors are required to have identification (either a national ID card or passport) on them at all times.

Personal Security

Overall crime rates in Athens are low, and it remains one of the safest capital cities in Europe. However, car break-ins are an increasing problem; try not to leave belongings on display. If you are robbed or assaulted, report the crime as soon as possible to the nearest police station or to the **tourist police**.

Pickpocketing in Athens and Thessaloníki is rife, particularly on crowded buses such as the X95 bus from the airport in Athens to Sýntagma. Monastiráki station on the Piraeus–Kifisiá metro line is also notorious as a spot targeted by thieves, as are Omonia Square and Omonia station. If you are coming from Piraeus (the port) towards the centre with luggage, alight at Néo Fáliro, walk the short distance to the SEF (Stathmós Irínis ke Filías) station, and continue into town on a tram. Your ticket will be valid for both journeys.

While the majority of the country holds conservative values, Greeks are generally accepting of all people, regardless of their race, gender or sexuality. Homosexuality was legalized in Greece in 1951, and gay marriage in 2024. The country's popularity as a gay destination goes hand in hand with the fact that LGBTQ+ rights are always improving. Athens' LGBTQ+ scene, which is centred around the fashionable Gazi neighbourhood, is where most of the city's gay and lesbian bars and clubs are situated. Rural communities and older generations tend to be less tolerant of public displays of affection from same-sex couples travelling together. If you feel unsafe or threatened, the **Safe Space Alliance** pinpoints your nearest place of refuge. Alternatively head for the nearest police station.

The ambulance service, fire brigade and police can be reached on the **European Emergency Number**. There are also dedicated lines for each of these emergency services. In the case of a medical emergency, another option that is available is **SOS Doctors**, a private organization on call 24/7, though be aware that its services are not covered under public healthcare. For non-emergencies, you can easily book appointments with doctors of all specialities. Prices vary but usually range from €30–50.

Responsible Tourism

The climate crisis is having a big impact on Greece at large, with heatwaves and wildfires becoming increasingly frequent during the extended summer months. If travelling during this period, consult the guidelines on the Civil Protection website and do your bit by careful disposing of cigarette butts and flammable litter.

DIRECTORY

PASSPORTS AND VISAS

Greek Ministry of Foreign Affairs
mfa.gr

ETIAS
etiasvisa.com

GOVERNMENT ADVICE

Australian Department of Foreign Affairs and Trade
smartraveller.gov.au

FCDO
gov.uk/foreign-travel-advice

US State Department
travel.state.gov

CUSTOMS INFORMATION

Greek Misistry of Tourism
mintour.gov.gr/en/archiki-english

INSURANCE

GHIC
nhs.uk

HEALTH

Doctor Anytime
doctoranytime.gr

Vrisko
vrisko.gr

PERSONAL SECURITY

Ambulance
166

Civil Protection
civilprotection.gov.gr

European Emergency Number
112

Fire
199

Police
100

Safe Space Alliance
safespacealliance.com

SOS Doctors
1016

Tourist Police
210 322 2230

Travellers with Specific Requirements

Although there have been massive improvements, Greece still has a long way to go to meet the needs of travellers with accessibility requirements. Some of the main attractions, such as the Acropolis and the Acropolis Museum, offer wheelchair access, but in general facilities are limited. All hotels by law must provide at least one room with disabled access, though compliance often is spotty. Metro stations in Athens are equipped with lifts that are large enough for those using wheelchairs, and most blue-and-white buses have middle-door ramps for wheelchairs. Major crosswalks have the kerb scooped out, but pips for sight-impaired pedestrians are rare. Visitors with disabilities enjoy free entry to state-run archaeological sites and museums.

Disability NOW is a useful directory for visitors with specific requirements travelling to Greece. It includes information for the visually impaired and deaf.

Time Zone

Greece operates on Eastern European Time (EET), which is two hours ahead of Greenwich Mean Time (GMT) and seven hours ahead of US Eastern Standard Time (EST). The clock moves forward one hour during daylight saving time, from the last Sunday in March until the last Sunday in October.

Money

Greece is a member of the Eurozone and uses the euro (€), which is divided into 100 cents (*lepta* in Greek). ATMs are widely available; surcharges depend on your bank. Also, foreign currencies can be exchanged for euros at bureaux de change in central Athens (a passport or ID card is required).

Major credit and debit cards are accepted in most shops and restaurants, while pre-paid currency cards and contactless payments are accepted in some. It is always worth carrying some cash.

It is customary to tip about ten per cent in restaurants, cafés and bars; when paying for a taxi, it is the norm to round the fare up to the nearest euro.

Electrical Appliances

Greece uses thick round-pin Schuko plugs of CEE 7/3 and 7/4 standards. The Schuko power points also accept the older, narrow-pin, unearthed Europlug CEE 7/16 or 7/17, but loosely. Electrical frequency and voltage in all cases is 230 V/50Hz. UK devices will need adaptors, while North American devices will need adaptors and voltage converters. Most electrical merchants in Athens offer plug adaptors.

Mobile Phones and Wi-Fi

Most restaurants, hotels and cafés in the city offer free Wi-Fi access. Syntagma Square, in the city centre, offers a free Wi-Fi hotspot.

Many visitors travelling to Greece with EU tariffs can use their devices without being affected by data roaming charges; instead they will be charged the same rates for data, SMS and voice calls as they would pay at home. Visitors from outside the EU can buy a local SIM card that they can use in an unlocked mobile phone to avoid having to pay roaming charges. Both the phone and the SIM card must be registered upon purchase, as part of anti-terrorism measures.

Postal Services

The main branch of Greece's **Hellenic Post (ELTA)** post office is on Syntagma Square and is open 7:30am–8:30pm Mon–Fri. Around the city, smaller post offices work 8am–2pm Mon–Fri. Letter boxes are bright yellow.

Weather

A Mediterranean climate means winters are cool and summers are sunny and hot, but you can always expect periods of rain. In the peak season (Jul–Aug), temperatures can soar to 40° C (104° F). The coldest months are Jan–Feb, when temperatures occasionally drop to 0° C (32° F) and snow is rare but not unknown. However, climate change is making temperatures unpredictable, and extreme summer heatwaves, with temperatures rising to 45°C (113°F), are becoming less uncommon.

Opening Hours

Office hours in Athens are generally 9am–5pm

Mon–Fri (some businesses close completely during August). Banks open 8am–2:30pm Mon–Thu and 8am–2pm Fri.

Shopping hours are a bit more complicated. Small, family-run stores typically open 9am– 2:30pm Mon and Wed; 9am–2pm and 5:30–8:30pm Tue and Thu–Fri; and 9am–3pm Sat. Supermarkets follow a different routine: Mon–Fri 8am–9pm, Sat 8am–8pm. Big Athenian department stores such as Attica and Notos adhere to the same schedule. However, there are no hard and fast rules, and opening hours tend to vary from store to store. Some stores close completely in August.

Many museums and some archaeological sites are closed on Tuesday, and some have earlier closings during winter. From September, many archaeological sites have earlier closing timings, which may change every two weeks as days grow shorter.

Most banks, stores and businesses are closed on public holidays.

> Situations can change quickly and unexpectedly. Always check before visiting attractions and hospitality venues for up-to-date opening hours and booking requirements.

Visitor Information

There are tourist information kiosks in Syntagma Square *(open 9am–8pm Mon–Fri, 9am–5pm Sat & Sun)* and in the arrivals area of the Athens Airport *(open 8am–8pm Mon–Fri, 9am–5pm Sat & Sun)*, which provide transport schedules and confirm timings of museums and sites. Business travellers can consult the **City of Athens Convention and Visitors Bureau** website. Both facilities give out maps and leaflets. The official website of the **Municipality of Athens** is useful, as is the **This is Athens** website, which is run by a number of official entities.

Local Customs

Modest attire (shoulders and knees should be covered by everyone) is required at Greek Orthodox churches and monasteries. Photography inside places of worship is often forbidden, so check first.

Language

Greek (Ellenika) is the official language, written using the Greek alphabet. Street signs are generally posted in both Greek and Latin characters. Most young people, especially those working in tourism, speak good English.

Taxes and Refunds

Usually included in the price, the top rate of FPA (Fóros Prostitheménis Axías) – the equivalent of VAT or sales tax – is 24 per cent in Greece, though taverna meals are assessed at 13 per cent. Visitors from outside the EU staying fewer than three months may claim this money back on purchases over €400. A Tax-Free form must be completed in the store, a copy of which is given to the customs authorities on departure, along with proof of purchase.

Accommodation

Athens has a wide range of places to sleep. Prestigious five-star hotels are found around Syntagma , while Plaka, Koukaki and Makrygianni have an array of mid-range boutique hotels and basic-but-comfortable pensions and B&Bs that make ideal bases for sightseeing, thanks to their proximity to the Acropolis. Psyrri and Monastiraki are also popular areas, with a mix of hip boutique hotels and hostels. Booking accommodation in advance is strongly recommended in the summer high season, when many visitors stop in Athens for a couple of nights before heading to the Greek islands.

DIRECTORY

TRAVELLERS WITH SPECIFIC REQUIREMENTS

Disability NOW
W disabled.gr

POSTAL SERVICES

ELTA (Hellenic Post)
W elta.gr

VISITOR INFORMATION

City of Athens Convention & Visitors Bureau
W athensconvention bureau.gr

Municipality of Athens
W cityofathens.gr

This is Athens
W thisisathens.org

Places to Stay

PRICE CATEGORIES
For a standard, double room per night (with breakfast if included), taxes and extra charges.

€ under €80 | €€ €80–200 | €€€ over €200

Luxury and High-End Hotels

Athenaeum Inter-Continental

MAP T2 ■ Syngrou 89–93, Neos Kosmos ■ 210 920 6000 ■ www.intercontinental.com ■ €€€
Well-equipped, modern and stylish, this hotel also has excellent business facilities that make it popular with executives, who also appreciate the gym, sauna, pool and shuttle to the city centre.

Four Seasons Astir Palace Hotel

MAP T3 ■ Apollonos 40, Vouliagmeni ■ 210 890 1000 ■ www.fourseasons.com/athens ■ €€€
The glamorous Four Seasons Astir Palace is the gold standard in beach-side luxury, offering private beaches, swimming pools and a host of dining options, including the Michelin-starred Pelagos.

St George Lycabettus

MAP F3 ■ Kleomenous 2, Kolonaki ■ 210 741 6000 ■ www.sgl.gr ■ €€
At this chic 154-room and 15-suite hotel built into the pine-scented slopes of Lykavittos Hill, full use is made of the rooftop, with an excellent restaurant, a swimming pool and a bar all sharing the great views. A minibus service will whisk you to Platia Syntagma.

Divani Apollon Palace & Thalasso

MAP T3 ■ Ag. Nikolaou 10 & Iliou, Vouliagmeni ■ 210 891 1100 ■ www.divani-apollonhotel.com ■ €€€
This is a vast seaside hotel that has spacious rooms adorned with oak furniture and marble bathrooms. The complex has a private beach, and there are also outdoor and indoor pools. The thalassotherapy centre located on the property is a major focus.

Divani Caravel

MAP G5 ■ Vasileos Alexandrou 2, Pangrati ■ 210 720 7000 ■ www.divanicaravel-hotel.com■ €€€
The lobby is decorated with antiques and marble, and the rooms are fitted out with every business amenity. Some 35 rooms have Acropolis views. There are bars and restaurants, and a rooftop garden with an indoor/outdoor pool, next to the gym/spa. A free shuttle takes you to Syntagma.

Electra Palace

MAP L4 ■ Navarhou Nikodimou 18–20, Plaka ■ 210 337 0000 ■ www.electrahotels.gr ■ €€€
This luxury hotel with opulent decor is arguably the best place to stay in Plaka. The rooftop pool, with Acropolis views, is a great place to cool off after a day of sightseeing.

The Electra Metropolis

MAP M3 ■ Mitropoleos 15 ■ 214 100 6200 ■ www.electrahotels.gr ■ €€€
A modernist landmark, this place is a smart retro-chic choice in the heart of downtown Athens. Guests can enjoy views of the Acropolis while dining on the rooftop. There's also a pool and gym on site.

Hotel Grande Bretagne

MAP M3 ■ Vas. Georgiou tou Protou 1, Syntagma ■ 210 333 0000 ■ www.grandebretagne.gr ■ €€€
This hotel exudes timeless luxury with its marble lobby and glittering chandeliers, along with 320 opulent rooms and suites, a rooftop restaurant and pool, and the fitness centre.

King George Hotel

MAP M3 ■ Vas. Georgiou tou Protou 3, Syntagma ■ 210 322 2210 ■ www.kinggeorgehotelathens.gr ■ €€€
A popular retreat among the rich and famous, this hotel has 102 rooms and suites, all with marble bathrooms and furnished with select antiques.

NJV Athens Plaza

MAP M3 ■ Vas. Georgiou tou Protou 2 & Stadiou ■ 210 335 2400 ■ www.njvathensplaza.gr ■ €€€
Smack in the city centre, this hotel has designer rooms with marble bathrooms, massage showers and Bulgari toiletries, plus a famously elegant lobby. Rooms on the eighth and ninth floors have great views of the Acropolis.

Boutique and Design Hotels

Coco Mat Athens

MAP P2 ■ Patriarhou oakeim 36, Kolonaki ■ 210 723 0000 ■ www. cocomatathens.com ■ €€€

The Greek mattress company Coco Mat runs several hotels showcasing its wonderful beds. This hotel has 39 rooms, all with wooden floors and fabrics in muted earthy tones, and bathrooms of grey marble or white tiles.

Emporikon Athens

MAP K3 ■ Aiolou 27A, Monastiraki ■ 693 016 1566 ■ www.emporikon athenshotel.com ■ €€

The Neo-Classical Emporikon Athens Hotel is set in a refurbished 19th-century landmark building located just off vibrant Platia Agia Irinis.

InnAthens

MAP L4 ■ Georgiou Souri 3 & Filellinon, Syntagma ■ 210 325 8555 ■ www. innathens.com ■ €€

Occupying a renovated Neo-Classical mansion, InnAthens has 22 rooms and suites with marble bathrooms and slick contemporary design. It centres on a peaceful courtyard, a short walk from Syntagma. The superb breakfast is made with local Greek produce.

O&B

MAP B3 ■ Leokoriou 7, Psyrri ■ 210 331 2940 ■ www.oandbhotel. com ■ €€

This welcoming hotel prides itself on personalized service. It has just 22 rooms and suites, with minimalist design and tones of cream and beige. The small bar-restaurant does a fantastic breakfast, as well as serves drinks and light meals all day. It is located on the boundary between Psyrri and Thisio districts, only a 20-minute walk from the Acropolis.

Pallas Athena

MAP C3 ■ Athinas 65, Athens ■ 210 325 0900 ■ www.grecotelpallas athena.com ■ €€€

A luxury boutique hotel, this is situated in the centre of the city and prides itself on its great art displays. The walls of its family rooms are decorated with fun murals and the loft suites are filled with contemporary art and sculpture. The hotel has an excellent restaurant with affordable set menus, and a tasty breakfast.

Periscope Hotel

MAP P2 ■ Haritos 22, Kolonaki ■ 210 729 7200 ■ www.donkeyhotels.gr/ periscope ■ €€€

A minimalist-style hotel, Periscope is located on a quiet street. The rooms get better on the higher floors in the building. The rooftop periscope (hence the name) scans the city and projects images in the lobby bistro.

Semiramis Hotel

MAP T2 ■ Harilaou Trikoupi 48, Kefalari, Kifissia ■ 210 628 4400 ■ www.donkeyhotels.gr/ semiramis ■ €€€

Dominant colours in this funky 51-room hotel, designed by Karim Rashid are orange, pink and lime-green. There's a heated outdoor pool and a fitness centre. A changing selection of contemporary art is displayed in the lobby.

AthensWas

MAP K5 ■ Dionysiou Areopagitou 5, Makrygianni ■ 210 924 9954 ■ www. athenswas.gr ■ €€

This 21-room hotel stands on a traffic-free promenade, a short walk from the Acropolis Museum. It's furnished with pieces by important 20th-century designers such as Le Corbusier and Eileen Gray, giving it a retro-chic vibe. The bathrooms are slick and spacious; the cooked-to-order breakfast is delicious. The rooftop restaurant at the hotel has the Acropolis immediately opposite it.

The Margi Hotel

MAP T3 ■ Litous 11, Vouliagmeni ■ 210 892 9000 ■ www.the-margi.gr ■ €€€

A five-minute walk from Vouliagmeni beach, this gem of a hotel has 89 rooms and suites, decorated in warm hues, with 19th-century antiques and marble bathrooms. Guests relax on poolside daybeds, and there is an excellent nouvelle cuisine restaurant on site.

New Hotel

MAP L4 ■ Filellinon 16, Syntagma ■ 210 327 3000 ■ www.donkeyhotels.gr/ newhotel ■ €€€

The art-filled New Hotel is close to Syntagma. Its 79 rooms feature bamboo floors and quirky recycled furniture created by the Campana brothers from Brazil. Cooked-to-order breakfast as well as the Sunday brunch are served in the New Taste restaurant, while later meals are served at the rooftop bar-bistro.

Mid-Range Hotels

Nefeli

MAP L4 ■ Yperidou 16, Plaka & Ag. Chatzimichali 2 ■ 210 322 8044 ■ www.hotel-nefeli.com ■ €

Located on a quiet pedestrian zone, Nefeli has 18 well maintained rooms; many have balconies. Breakfasts at the hotel are very good and the staff is friendly.

Acropolis Select

MAP C6 ■ Falirou 37–9, Koukaki ■ 210 921 1610 ■ www.acropolis elect.gr ■ €

One of the best deals in town: for only a little more than a budget hotel, you get a stylish lobby, a skylit restaurant, comfortable rooms, satellite TV, business amenities and Acropolis views. It is a short walk from most of the tourist sights.

A for Athens

MAP J3 ■ Miaouli 2–4, Monastiraki ■ 210 324 4244 ■ www.aforathens.com ■ €€€

This boutique hotel with a contemporary design ethos and 35 rooms (including family quads) is just across from the Acropolis, so guests enjoy unique views of this ancient monument even while they take a shower.

Athens Center Square

MAP J2 ■ Aristogeitonos 15, Monastiraki ■ 210 322 2706 ■ www.athens centersquarehotel.gr ■ €€

Located downtown opposite the Varvakios Central Market, this friendly, welcoming hotel has 54 colour-themed rooms with wooden floors, and a rooftop terrace with views of the Acropolis and Lykavittos Hill. The price includes a generous buffet breakfast.

Central Hotel

MAP L3 ■ Apollonos 21, Syntagma ■ 210 323 4350 ■ www.central hotel.gr ■ €€

Modern, minimalist and smart, the Central is one of the most reasonably priced hotels for its quality and location. Relax in the rooftop whirlpool with a view of the Acropolis and the mountains beyond.

Hermes

MAP L3 ■ Apollonos 19, Syntagma ■ 210 322 2706 ■ www.hermes hotel.gr ■ €€

The Hermes has 45 rooms with wooden floors and cheerful, contemporary design. Some of the rooms are interconnected, which makes them ideal for families. There is also a playroom for small kids. A large buffet breakfast, based on typical Greek produce, or a pre-dawn service for early departers, is included.

Herodion

MAP C6 ■ Rovertou Galli 4, Makrygianni ■ 214 402 5700 ■ www.herodion.gr ■ €€€

In a quiet neighbourhood just below the Acropolis, this attractive, modern hotel has comfortable if small rooms. It does manage to score the highest for its common areas: a ground-floor breakfast area with a landscaped conservatory, and a roof garden with two whirlpools, eyefuls of the Acropolis plus yoga and massage on request.

Hotel Plaka

MAP K3 ■ Kapnikareas 7 & Mitropoleos, Monastiraki ■ 210 322 2706 ■ www.plakahotel.gr ■ €€

This hotel represents excellent value – for its unbeatable location between Plaka and the shopping street of Ermou, as well as for its warm and simple but stylish rooms in three grades. The roof garden offers a view of the Acropolis.

Philippos Hotel

MAP K6 ■ Mitseon 3, Makrygianni ■ 210 922 3611 ■ www.philippos hotel.gr ■ €€

In a peaceful residential side street, close to the Acropolis Museum, the Herodion's sister hotel is welcoming, peaceful and comfortable. The 50 rooms and suites are light and airy – most have balconies, some have Acropolis views. The continental breakfast is adequate, and there are rooftop and atrium bistros.

Ava

MAP L5 ■ Lysikratous 9–11, Plaka ■ 210 325 9000 ■ www.avahotel.gr ■ €€€

Known for its high service standards, this hotel has smaller units for couples and big suites for families of four. Some of the higher units have oblique views of the Acropolis.

Budget Hotels and Hostels

Art Gallery Hotel

MAP C6 ■ Erechthiou 5, Koukaki ■ 210 923 8376 ■ www.artgallery hotel.gr ■ €

Priciest in the budget options, this hotel is a

short walk from the Acropolis. It has wooden parquet floors and art in every room, though three bathrooms are down the hall. Off-season monthly rates are low, and breakfast is extra.

Athens Backpackers

MAP L5 ■ Makri 12, Makrygianni ■ 210 922 4044 ■ www.backpackers.gr ■ €

At this hostel, there are dorms with three to six beds, and the ensuing social life makes it hugely popular. They also have an annexe, Athens Studios.

Athens Choice

MAP C2 ■ Veranzerou 45, Omonia ■ 210 523 8738 ■ www.athenschoice.com ■ €

This hostel has a modern minimalist look in greys and charcoal. Available room types include private rooms and shared dorms (sleeping four). There is a bar, TV lounge and laundry service, plus breakfast is included. It's a five-minute walk from the Omonia metro station; in addition, Exarhia and the National Archaeological Museum are not too far away.

City Circus Hostel

MAP J2 ■ Sarri 16, Psyrri ■ 213 023 7244 ■ www.citycircus.gr ■ €

In a renovated Neo-Classical mansion with frescoed ceilings, wrought-iron balconies and vintage furniture, retro-chic City Circus is a five-minute walk from Monastiraki metro station. It has private doubles and shared dorms sleeping four, six or eight, a restaurant and a roof terrace with a view of the Acropolis.

When in Athens Hostel

MAP D2 ■ Valtetsiou 17, Exarchia ■ 211 750 3244 ■ www.wheninathenshostel.com ■ €

Wooden, screened bunk beds make for a comfortable, budget-friendly stay in this restored aristocratic building with modern amenities. Note, the bathrooms, kitchen and lounge areas are shared.

Hotel Phaedra

MAP L5 ■ Cherefontos 16, Plaka ■ 210 323 8461 ■ www.hotelphaedra.com ■ €

Known for its welcoming staff, this 21-room family-run hotel features balconies overlooking a Byzantine church or the Acropolis. The rooms are tastefully appointed, and some have private bathrooms that are located across the hall. The rooftop terrace of the Phaedra is a great place for its magnificent views.

Marble House Pension

MAP B6 ■ Alley off Anastasiou Zinni 35, Koukaki ■ 210 923 4058 ■ www.marblehouse.gr ■ €

A favourite of students as well as artists, and very peacefully set on a dead-end lane, Marble House has clean, simple rooms and a friendly atmosphere. It offers discounted tours and monthly rates in the off season. Be aware that some of the rooms here share a bathroom down the hall. Breakfast is extra, and service from the managing family is kind. It is mandatory to make reservations in advance of your stay.

Orion-Dryades

MAP D2 ■ Anexarteslas 6, by Kallidromiou and Benaki ■ 210 330 2387 ■ www.orion-dryades.com ■ €

These Siamese-Twin co-managed hotels, sitting peacefully above the buzz of Exárhia on Stgrefi Hill, are a long-standing, safe favourite for those seeking budget accommodation. Breakfast is served at the Orion, where the reception is located. There is a stiff climb uphill, so take a taxi if heavily laden.

Tempi Hotel

MAP J2 ■ Aiolou 29, Monastiraki ■ 210 321 3175 ■ www.tempihotel.gr ■ €

This family-run budget hotel is located near Platía Agias Irinis, and is also close to major attractions. The rooms are simple and comfortable, and 14 of the 24 rooms have en suite bathrooms. A roof terrace, a communal kitchen and the facility of free luggage storage are major pluses.

Athens Studios

MAP K6 ■ Veïkou 3A, Makrygianni ■ 210 923 5811 ■ www.athensstudios.gr ■ €€

Co-managed with Athens Backpackers, this is even closer to the Acropolis Museum. Room types include private studios and apartments (sleeping from two to six) that are ideal for couples or families and come with fully equipped kitchens and small en suite bathrooms. Shared dorms that accommodate up to six people are also an option. The tariff includes a continental breakfast.

***For a key to hotel price categories** see p144*

High-End Hotels Outside Athens

Kastalia Boutique Hotel

MAP Q1 ■ Vasileos Pavlou and Friderikis 13, Delphi ■ 226 508 2205 ■ www.kastaliahotel.gr ■ €

Set in a Neo-Classical mansion, this boutique hotel is close to Delphi's archaeological site. It has 28 rooms and suites, as well as a lounge with an open fireplace. Breakfast is served on the stone terrace, with views of the Plistos gorge and the sea.

Bratsera

MAP S4 ■ Tompazi 2 by the harbour, Hydra ■ 229 805 3971 ■ Mar–Oct ■ www.bratserahotel.com ■ €€€

This hotel housed in a former sponge factory is one of the most charming places to stay on Hydra. The best units are junior suites, some with private terraces. There are also quads for families. The very deep pool (where sponges were rinsed at one time) is the only one of its kind in town.

Orloff Hotel

MAP S4 ■ Rafalia 9, Platia Nikolaou Votsi, Hydra port ■ 229 805 2564 ■ www.orloff.gr ■ €€€

All the rooms at Hydra's first boutique hotel are unique in layout; some overlook the town, others the breakfast courtyard. The premium suite fits parents and two kids.

Anima Deluxe Suites

MAP R3 ■ 25 Martiou, Evaggelistrias, Nafplio ■ 2752 099 221 ■ €€

These chic suites not only offer excellent value for money, but also make a good base for exploring Nafplio. All rooms have private patios and there's a shared pool. There's also optional breakfast, free street parking and concierge service.

Elatos Resort & Health Club

MAP R1 ■ Itamos, nr Arachova ■ 223 406 1162 ■ www.elatosresort.gr ■ €€€

Greece's only alpine resort is set in a pine forest at the edge of Parnassos National Park. All 40 chalets have two to three bedrooms, kitchens, fireplaces and verandas. The central buildings offer a fully equipped health club, bar and restaurant.

Grand Resort Lagonissi

MAP T3 ■ 40th km on the Athens–Sounio road, Lagonissi ■ 229 107 6000 ■ www.lagonissiresort.gr ■ €€€

This vast resort complex spreads out over its own peninsula between Sounio and Vouliagmeni. The resort encompasses 16 beaches, a range of sea-front suites and lavish villas that have their own pools. There are also a host of restaurants and organized activities.

Grecotel Cape Sounio

MAP T3 ■ 67th km on the Athens–Sounio Rd ■ 229 206 9700 ■ www.grecotel.com/capesounio ■ €€€

Offering all the mod cons you would expect in its bungalows and villas, this hotel is set on a verdant hillside, with spectacular views of the sea and the Temple of Poseidon.

Orloff Resort

Spetses ■ 229 807 5444 ■ www.orloffresort.com ■ €€€

This stylish boutique hotel is set in a 19th-century mansion with an outdoor pool. The 19 rooms, studios and apartments combine traditional Greek architecture with modern and minimalist design.

Thermae Sylla Spa and Wellness Hotel

MAP S1 ■ Edipsos, North Évia ■ 222 606 0100 ■ www.thermaesylla.gr ■ €€€

One of the best spas in Greece, the Thermae Sylla offers treatments featuring local restorative mineral-laden spring waters and a thermal pool, as well as a wide array of beauty and relaxation treatments. The Belle Epoque external architecture has been preserved; but the rooms and treatment areas are fully modern.

Wyndham Poseidon Resort

MAP R2 ■ Loutraki Korinthias, Loutraki ■ 274 406 7938 ■ www.wyndhamloutrakiresort.com ■ €€€

This resort has a small private beach and extensive gardens, as well as sporting, spa and conference facilities. Options for accommodation comprise 13 grades of suites, which range from a junior suite with a garden view to a presidential seafront suite; most of the suites can accommodate four people. All suites share wooden flooring but not much else, so be sure that you read the room descriptions carefully.

Mid and Budget Outside Athens

Aeginitiko Archontiko

MAP S3 ■ Thomaidou 1 & Agiou Nikolaou, Egina Town ■ 2297 024 968 ■ www.aeginitiko-archontiko.gr ■ €

A 19th-century mansion, this has painted ceilings upstairs, a parlour with stained-glass windows, and a garden courtyard. A dozen rooms are small and clean.

Alkyoni

MAP S3 ■ Skala, south end on clifftop, Angistri ■ 229 709 1377 ■ www.alkyoni-agistri.gr ■ €

With a tranquil location, this hotel has flagstoned, ground-floor doubles and better specced rooms upstairs for families. The terrace restaurant is one of the better places to eat on Angistri.

Byron

MAP R3 ■ Platonos 2, Platia Agiou Spyridona, Nafpliou ■ 275 202 2351 ■ www.byronhotel.gr ■ €

The first of Nafplion's boutique hotels, this is still one of the best. Many rooms overlook a domed Ottoman hammam; some have balconies. The units are scattered over two buildings. The breakfasts are very good.

John & George Hotel

MAP R4 ■ Vas. Hali St 8, Tolo ■ 275 205 9868 ■ €

This superb family-run hotel has comfortable, modern rooms, a lovely pool, stunning views and serves an excellent breakfast. Tolo is a charming fishing village with a long beach, many good tavernas by the sea and a friendly atmosphere. Close to Nafplio, Mycenae and Epidavros, it's a convenient place to stay while exploring this historic region of the Peloponnese.

Likoria

MAP R1 ■ West edge of town, Venizelou, Arachova ■ 226 703 1180 ■ www.likoria.gr ■ €

This comfortable hotel is open in summer and winter. With sauna and hammam, it is aimed at skiers. The best rooms have a view and a fireplace. It's a good choice for drivers as street parking is possible here, unlike in central Arahova.

Orfeas

MAP Q1 ■ Ifigenias Syngrou 35, Delphi ■ 2265 082 077 ■ €

A small, friendly, family-run hotel, this is on a quiet upper street away from the noisy main thoroughfares but still walkable to almost everything. Breakfast here is better than the star category (2) would suggest. Top-floor rooms are best for appointment and views.

Archontiko Art Hotel

MAP Q1 ■ Hillside beyond Hirolakkas cove, Galaxidi ■ 2265 042 292 ■ www.archontikoarthotel.gr ■ €€

The eight themed rooms here sound a little kitschy but most manage to work. The "Bridal" has a huge canopy bed draped with sheer white linen; the "At Sea" is decorated like a boat; while adventurous couples often choose the "Conception", featuring a round bed and mirrored ceiling. When not enjoying their rooms, guests can stroll in the garden.

Hotel Ganimede

MAP Q1 ■ Nikolaou Gourgouri 20, Galaxidi ■ 226 504 1328 ■ www.ganimede.gr ■ €€

This 19th-century mansion has six simple but elegant doubles, a modern family suite across the courtyard garden, and another one that is more remote, along with studios. The Papalexis family are excellent hosts, and the breakfasts feature homemade jams and bread straight from their family bakery. Reservations are mandatory all year, more so on weekends.

Klymeni Traditional Homes

MAP R3 ■ Eparchiaki Odos Nafpliou - Frouriou Palamidiou ■ 275 209 6194 ■ www.klymeni.gr ■ €€

Offering accommodation in a range of rustic-chic studios, bungalows and apartments built of local natural stone, Klymeni is set in gardens with a barbecue, a hot tub and a children's play area. Surrounded by peaceful rural farmland, it's 1.5 km (1 mile) southeast of town, off the castle road.

Pension Marianna

MAP R3 ■ Ilia Potamianou 9, Nafplio ■ 2752 024 256 ■ www.hotelmarianna.gr ■ €€

Located in the car-free Old Town of Nafplio, this welcoming inn is quaint and romantic. Centred around a lovely courtyard, its 20 rooms are in warm shades of yellow, orange and red. A homemade 'organic' breakfast (extra charge) is served on a rooftop patio that is right below the fortress, with lovely views over the town to the Argolid Gulf.

***For a key to hotel price categories** see p144*

General Index

Page numbers in **bold** refer to main entries

Acknowledgments

This edition updated by
Contributor Amber Charmei
Senior Editors Dipika Dasgupta, Keith Drew
Senior Art Editor Vinita Venugopal
Project Editor Anuroop Sanwalia
Editor Nandini Desiraju
Editorial Assistant Catrina Conway
Art Editor Sulagna Das
Assistant Picture Research Administrator Manpreet Kaur
Rights and Permissions Specialist Priya Singh
Deputy Picture Research Manager Virien Chopra
Senior Cartographer Subhashree Bharati
Cartography Manager Suresh Kumar
Pre-production Coordinator Tanveer Zaidi
Pre-production Designers Rajdeep Singh, Rohit Rojal
Senior Production Controller Kariss Ainsworth
Managing Editor Beverly Smart
Editorial Director Hollie Teague
Senior Managing Art Editor Priyanka Thakur
Art Director Maxine Pedliham
Publishing Director Georgina Dee

DK would like to thank the following for their contribution to the previous editions:Hilary Bird, Blue Island Publishing London, Coral Davenport, Marc Dubin, Jane Foster, Cordelia Madden, Clare Peel and Marisa Tejada.

Commissioned Photography Courtesy of ARF/TAP (Archaeological Receipts Fund), Nigel Hicks, Courtesy of Kori 69b, Rob Reichenfeld, Rough Guides/Chris Christoforo, Rough Guides/Michelle Grant

The publisher would like to thank the following for their kind permission to reproduce their photographs:

Key: a-above; b-below/bottom; c-centre; f-far; l-left; r-right; t-top

123RF.com: Milan Gonda 77br; gzach 34br; Maxim Krivoshein 123tl; Stefanos Kyriazis 77t.

4Corners: Mel Manser 13crb; Gianluca Santoni 47tl, 87cl.

Alamy Stock Photo: age fotostock/Gonzalo Azumendi 96br, /Alvaro Leiva 17tc; Alpineguide 2tl, 8-9; A. Amsel 79tl; Art Directors & TRIP/ Helene Rogers 129cr; The Art Archive/Gianni Dagli Orti 53cl; charistoone-travel 31clb; Richard Cummins 108cla; Ian Dagnall 17crb; dpa picture alliance 55br; Fine Arts/ INTERFOTO 102bl; Kirk Fisher 109tr; funkyfood London - Paul Williams 3tl, 4t; Glyn Genin 103cl; Milan Gonda 24-5c, 74-5; Greek Photonews 12cl; Peter Grumann 63b; Terry Harris 61cl, 70tl, 72cl, 84br, 104cla; Hector Christiaen 98cl; Chris Hellier 4clb; hemis.fr/ Guiziou Franck 43tr, Paule Seux 4cr; Heritage Image Partnership Ltd/Fine Art Images 26cl, / Sites & Photos 25tl; Peter Horree 23crb, 49t; Imageplotter 18crb; IML Image Group 31br, / Velissarios Voutsas 33br; INTERFOTO 57cla; Jon Arnold Images Ltd / Peter Adams 107cr; Art Kowalsky 4cla; Lanmas 40b; Hercules Milas 4b, 34-5, 34cla, 48, 110cr, 110-1tc, 116crb, 129t; nagelestock.com 7tr; Numismatic Museum of Athens 93br; Steve Outram 72tr; Lefteris Partsalis / Xinhua 66br; Nikos Pavlakis 70b, 94b; Brian Ormerod Photographer 15b; Davide D. Phstock 62; Prisma Archivo 19cr; Prisma Bildagentur AG/ Schultz Reinhard 41cla; Natasa Savic 97cr; Sklifas Steven 11cla, 30br, 30-1, 37tr; Aristidis Vafeiadakis 49br; Elias Verdi 43clb; Ken Welsh 4crb; Jan Wlodarczyk 2tr, 38-9, 102t; World History Archive 52t; ZUMA Press, Inc. 51br.

An Club, Solomou: 99t.

AWL Images: Hemis 3tr, 120-121, 134-5; Jane Sweeney 28-9, 60b.

Benaki Museum Athens: 11tr, 26crb, 27cla, 27crb; Antonis Katrakazis 105t.

Booze Cooperative: 91br.

Bridgeman Images: Epigraphical Museum, Archaelogical Museum, Athens, De Agostini Picture Library/Archivio J. Lange 93c.

Corbis: Richard Cummins 71tr, 109br; Demotix/ Kostas Pikoulas 73cl; EPA/Yannis Kolesidis 55cr, /Orestis Panagiotou 77cl, 93tl; Macduff Everton 95cl; Keystone/Georgios Kefalas14tl; Leemage 10c; Francis G. Mayer 52bl; Daniella Nowitz 33tl; Thierry Orban 42t; Ted Spiegel 50crb.

Dreamstime.com: Absente 118bc; Abxyz 40c; Anastasios71 6cl; Artistique7 17cr; Jennifer Barrow 10cla; Pavla Bartonova 30clb; Sergio Bertino 20crb; Daniel Boiteau 36br; Boris Breytman 122tl; Joaquin Ossorio Castillo 44clb; Trinuch Chareon 133c; Corluc 54tl; Digitaldave 115br; Dimaberkut 100tr, 104br; Edwardgerges 15tl, 96tl, 132bl; Elgreko74 45tl, 63cla; Alexandre Fagundes De Fagundes 49cl, 76tl; Foodio 65cl; Gelia 116tl; Dimitrios Giannopoulos 130tl; Gmoulart 118t; Milan Gonda 84cla, 86b, 110bl; Stoyan Haytov 117br; Theodoros Ikramidis 24br; Imagin.gr Photography 12tr, 124tl; Gabriela Insuratelu 128tl, 131cl; Ivandzyuba 113tr; Kmiragaya 50ca; Dimitris Kolyris 11crb, 18ca; Martin Konečný 90cb; Bo Li 12bc; Littlewormy 10ca; Lornet 60tl; Galina Mikhalishina 61tr; Predrag Milosavljevic 64bl; Milosk50 78b; Minadezhda 64c; Niradj 64tr; Odua 83crb; Pantelis V. 114c; Lefteris Papaulakis 10crb, 11bl, 16-7, 20-1, 53br, 46b, 88tl, 115tl, 126bl; Emmanouil Pavlis 19b, 35tl; Photogolfer 117tl; Photostella 71cl, 85tl; Rhombur 36-7; Rosshelen 16bl; Sborisov 12-3, 101clb; Jozef Sedmak 47crb; Nikolai Sorokin 45b, 113cb, 124b; George Tsartsianidis 65tl; Valery109 24cla; Vitaliybilyak 132cra; Bruce Whittingham 68tr,130b; Wirestock 68clb; Angel Yordanov 123b.

Epikouros Restaurant - Taverna: 119cr.

Getty Images: AFP PHOTO/Louisa Gouliamaki 21bc; Allan Baxter 4cl, 58-9; DEA /A. Garozzo 79clb, /G. Nimatallah 18cl, /G. Dagli Orti 21crb; Lonely Planet Images 78cla; Slow Images 86cla; George Tsafos 88crb; Universal Images Group 11cr.

Getty Images / iStock: E+ / Guven Ozdemir 1.

Nicholas P Goulandris Foundation - Museum of Cycladic Art: 10bl, 22cla, 22c, 22br, 22-3, 23ca, 56tl.

HELLENIC FESTIVAL S.A.: 72br.

Hytra: Kaplanidis Yirgos 67cl.

Getty Images/iStock: efesenko 125cla.

Martinos Antiques: 89tr.

Melissinos Art - The Poet

© naked summers: Chrisitina Mandilari 97tl.

Oinoscent: Katherine Whittaker (Instagram ID: kaywhitt07) 106.

Rakadiko Stoa Kouvelou: 112br.

Restaurant Spondi: 67tl.

Rififi: 67br.

Robert Harding Picture Library: Massimo Pizzotti 20bl; Silwen Randebrock 26tr.

Photo Scala, Florence: 32cr; DeAgostini Picture Library/Veneranda Biblioteca Ambrosiana 55cl.

Shutterstock.com: De Agostini/G. Dagli Orti 92tl; Sharok Hatami 41br; Vangelis_ Vassalakis 127cl.

Six D.O.G.S: 91tl

Skoumoky: 81t.

Strofi Athenian Restaurant: 83cla.

SuperStock: LatitudeStock/Capture Ltd 73tr.

The New Acropolis Museum: Giorgos Vitsaropoulos 82b.

WeArePress: 66cla.

Cover

Front and spine: **Getty Images:** Moment / Alexander Spatari. Back: **AWL Images:** Ken Scicluna cla; **Dreamstime.com:** Jun Tang tl, Napa735 tr.

Pull Out Map Cover

AWL Images: Getty Images: Moment / Alexander Spatari.

*As a guide to abbreviations in visitor information blocks: **Adm** = admission charge; **D** = dinner.*

MIX
Paper | Supporting responsible forestry
FSC www.fsc.org FSC™ C018179

This book was made with Forest Stewardship Council™ certified paper – one small step in DK's commitment to a sustainable future.
Learn more at
www.dk.com/uk/information/sustainability

Penguin Random House

First edition 2004

Published in Great Britain by Dorling Kindersley Limited, 20 Vauxhall Bridge Road, London SW1V 2SA

The authorised representative in the EEA is Dorling Kindersley Verlag GmbH. Arnulfstr. 124, 80636 Munich, Germany

Published in the United States by DK Publishing, 1745 Broadway, 20th Floor, New York, NY 10019, USA

26 27 28 29 10 9 8 7 6 5 4 3 2 1

A CIP catalogue record is available from the British Library.

A catalogue record for this book is available from the Library of Congress.

ISSN 1479-344X
ISBN 978 0 2417 9032 8

Printed and bound in China

www.dk.com

Phrase Book

In an Emergency

Help!	**Voithia!**	*vo-ee-theea*
Stop!	**Stamatíste!**	*sta-ma-tee-steh*
Call a doctor!	**Fonáxte éna giatró!**	*fo-nak-steh e-na ya-tro*
Call an ambulance/ the police/ fire brigade!	**Kaléste to asthenofóro/tin astynomía/tin pyrosvestikí!**	*ka-le-steh to as-the-no-fo-ro teen a-sti-no-the mia/ teen pee-ro-zve-stee-kee!*
Where is the nearest telephone/ hospital/ pharmacy?	**Poú eínai to plisiéstero tiléfono/ nosokomeío/ farmakeío?**	*poo ee-ne to plee-see-e-ste-ro tee-le-pho-no/ no-so-ko-mee-o/ far-ma-kee-o*

Communication Essentials

Yes	**Nai**	*neh*
No	**Ohi**	*o-hee*
Please	**Parakaló**	*pa-ra-ka-lo*
Thank you	**Efharistó**	*ef-ha-ree-sto*
You are welcome	**Parakaló**	*pa-ra-ka-lo*
OK/alright	**Endáxei**	*en-dak-zee*
Excuse me	**Me synchoreíte**	*me seen-cho-ree-teh*
Hello	**Giá sas**	*yeea sas*
Goodbye	**Andío**	*an-dee-o*
Good morning	**Kaliméra**	*ka-lee-me-ra*
Good night	**Kalinýhta**	*ka-lee-neech-ta*
Morning	**Proí**	*pro-ee*
Afternoon	**Apógevma**	*a-po-yev-ma*
Evening	**Vrádi**	*vrath-i*
This morning	**Símera to proí**	*see-me-ra to pro-ee*
Yesterday	**Chthés**	*chthes*
Today	**Símera**	*see-me-ra*
Tomorrow	**Avrio**	*av-ree-o*
Here	**Edó**	*ed-o*
There	**Ekeí**	*e-kee*
What?	**Tí?**	*tee*
Why?	**Giatí?**	*ya-tee*
Where?	**Poú?**	*poo*
How?	**Pós?**	*pos*
Wait!	**Perímene!**	*pe-ree-me-neh*
How are you?	**Tí káneis?**	*tee ka-nees*
Very well, thank you.	**Poly kalá, efharistó.**	*po-lee ka-la, ef-cha-ree-sto*
How do you do?	**Pós eíste?**	*pos ees-te*
Pleased to meet you.	**Hero polý.**	*che-ro po-lee*
What is your name?	**Pós légeste?**	*pos le-ye-ste*
Where is/are…?	**Poú eínai…?**	*poo ee-ne*
How far is it to…?	**Póso apéhei…?**	*po-so a-pe-chee*
How do I get to…?	**Pós boró na páo…?**	*pos bo-ro na pa-o*
Do you speak English?	**Miláte Angliká?**	*mee-la-te an-glee-ka*
I understand.	**Katalavaíno.**	*ka-ta-la-ve-no*
I don't understand.	**Den katalavaíno.**	*then ka-ta-la-ve-no*
Could you speak slowly?	**Miláte lígo pio argá parakaló?**	*mee-la-te lee-go pyo ar-ga pa-ra-ka-lo*
I'm sorry.	**Me synhoreíte.**	*me seen-cho-ree-teh*

Does anyone have a key?	**Ehei kanis kleidí?**	*e-chee ka-ne-es klee-dee*

Useful Words

big	**Megálo**	*me-ga-lo*
small	**Mikró**	*mi-kro*
hot	**Zestó**	*zes-to*
cold	**Krýo**	*kree-o*
good	**Kaló**	*ka-lo*
bad	**Kakó**	*ka-ko*
enough	**Arketá**	*ar-ke-ta*
well	**Kalá**	*ka-la*
open	**Anoihtá**	*a-neech-ta*
closed	**Kleistá**	*klee-sta*
left	**Aristerá**	*a-ree-ste-ra*
right	**Dexiá**	*dek-see-a*
straight on	**Efthía**	*ef-thee-a*
between	**Anámesa / Metaxý**	*a-na-me-sa/ me-tak-see*
on the corner of…	**Sti gonía tou…**	*stee go-nee-a too*
near	**Kondá**	*kon-da*
far	**Makriá**	*ma-kree-a*
up	**Epáno**	*e-pa-no*
down	**Káto**	*ka-to*
early	**Norís**	*no-rees*
late	**Argá**	*ar-ga*
entrance	**I ísodos**	*ee ee-so-thos*
exit	**I éxodos**	*ee e-kso-dos*
toilet occupied/ engaged	**I toualétes / Kateiliméni**	*ee too-a-le-tes ka-tee-lee-me-nee*
unoccupied	**Eléftheri**	*e-lef-the-ree*
free/no charge	**Doreán**	*tho-re-an*
in/out	**Mésa/ Exo**	*me-sa/ek-so*

Making a Telephone Call

Where is the nearest public telephone?	**Poú vrísketai o plisiésteros tilefonikós thálamos?**	*poo vrees-ke-teh o plee-see-e-ste-ros tee-le-fo-ni-kos tha-la-mos*
I would like to place a long-distance call.	**Tha íthela na káno éna yperastikó tilefónima.**	*tha ee-the-la na ka-no e-na ee-pe-ra-sti-ko tee-le-fo-nee-ma.*
I would like to reverse the charges.	**Tha íthela na chreóso to tilefónima ston paralípti.**	*tha ee-the-la na chre-o-so to tee-le-fo-nee-ma ston pa-ra-lep-tee*
I will try again later.	**Tha xanatilefoníso argótera.**	*tha ksa-na-tee-le-fo-ni-so ar-go-te-ra*
Can I leave a message?	**Mporeíte na tou afísete éna mínyma?**	*bo-ree-te na too a-fee-se-teh e-na mee-nee-ma*
Could you speak up a little please?	**Miláte dynatótera, parakaló?**	*mee-la-teh dee-na-to-te-ra, pa-ra-ka-lo*
Hold on.	**Periménete.**	*pe-ri-me-ne-teh*
local call	**Topikó tilefónima**	*to-pi-ko tee-le-fo-nee-ma*
phone box/ kiosk	**O tilefonikós thálamos**	*o tee-le-fo-ni-kos tha-la-mos*
phone card	**I tilekárta**	*ee tee-le-kar-ta*

Shopping

How much does this cost?	**Póso kánei?**	*po-so ka-nee*

I would like…	**Tha íthela…**	*tha ee-the-la*
Do you have…?	**Ehete…?**	*e-che-teh*
I am just looking.	**Aplós koitáo.**	*a-plos kee-ta-o*
Do you take credit cards	**Décheste pistotikés kártes**	*the-ches-teh pee-sto-tee-kes kar-tes*
What time do you open/close?	**Póte anoígete/ klínete?**	*po-teh a-nee-ye-teh/ klee-ne-teh*
Can you ship this overseas?	**Boreíte na to steílete sto exoterikó?**	*bo-ree-teh na to stee-le-teh sto e-xo-te-ree-ko*
This one.	**Aftó edó.**	*af-to e-do*
That one.	**Ekeíno.**	*e-kee-no.*
expensive	**Akrivó**	*a-kree-vo*
cheap	**Fthinó**	*fthee-no*
size	**To mégethos**	*to me-ge-thos*
white	**Lefkó**	*lef-ko*
black	**Mávro**	*mav-ro*
red	**Kókkino**	*ko-kee-no*
yellow	**Kítrino**	*kee-tree-no*
green	**Prásino**	*pra-see-no*
blue	**Mple**	*bleh*

Sightseeing

tourist information	**O EOT**	*o E-OT*
tourist police	**I touristikí astynomía**	*ee too-rees-tee-kee a-stee-no-mee-a*
closed on public holidays	**kleistó tis argíes**	*klee-sto tees aryee-es*

Transport

When does the … leave?	**Póte févgei to…?**	*po-teh fev-yee to*
Where is the bus stop?	**Poú eínai i stási tou leoforeíou?**	*poo ee-neh ee sta-see too le-o-fo-ree-oo*
Is there a bus to…?	**Ypárhei leoforeío gia…?**	*ee-par-chee le-o-fo-ree-o yia*
ticket office	**Ekdotíria isitiríon**	*Ek-tho-tee-reea ee-see-tee-ree-on*
return ticket	**Isitírio me epistrofí**	*ee-see-tee-ree-o meh e-pee-stro-fee*
single journey	**Apló isitírio**	*a-plo ee-see-tee-reeo*
bus station	**O stathmós tou KTEL**	*o stath-mos too KTEL*
bus ticket	**Isitírio leoforíou**	*ee-see-tee-ree-o leo-fo-ree-oo*
trolley bus	**To trólley**	*to tro-le-ee*
port	**To limáni**	*to lee-ma-nee*
train/metro	**To tréno**	*to tre-no*
railway station	**sidirodromikós stathmós**	*see-thee-ro-thro-mee-kos stath-mos*
scooter/ motorbike	**papaki/ To mihanáki**	*pa-pa-kee/ to-mee-cha-na-kee*
bicycle	**To podílato**	*to po-thee-la-to*
taxi	**To taxí**	*to tak-see*
airport	**To aerodrómio**	*to a-e-ro-thro-mee-o*
ferry	**To "ferry-boat"**	*to fe-ree-bot*
hydrofoil	**To delfíni/ To ydroptérygo**	*to del-fee-nee/ To ee-throp-te-ree-go*
catamaran	**To katamarán**	*to catamaran*
for hire	**Enoikiázontai**	*e-nee-kya-zon-deh*

Staying in a Hotel

Do you have a vacant room?	**Ehete domátia?**	*e-he-teh tho-ma-tee-a*
I have a reservation.	**Echo kánei krátisi.**	*e-cho ka-nee kra-tee-see.*
double room with double bed	**Díklino me dipló kreváti**	*thee-klee-no meh thee-plo kre-va-tee*
twin room	**Díklino me moná krevátia**	*thee-klee-no meh mo-na kre-vat-ya*
single room	**Monóklino**	*mo-no-klee-no*
room with a bath	**Domátio me mpánio**	*tho-ma-tee-o meh ban-yo*
shower	**To douz**	*To dooz*
bathtub	**Baniéra**	*Ban-yeh-ra*
porter	**O portiéris**	*o por-tye-rees*
key	**To kleidí**	*to klee-dee*
room with a sea view/balcony	**Domátio me théa sti thálassa/ balkóni**	*tho-ma-tee-o meh the-a stee tha-la-sa/bal-ko-nee*
Does the price include breakfast?	**To proïnó symperi-lamvánetai stin timí?**	*to pro-ee-no seem-be-ree-lam-va-ne-teh steen tee-me*

Eating Out

Have you got a table?	**Ehete trapézi?**	*e-che-te tra-pe-zee*
I want to reserve a table.	**Thélo na kratíso éna trapézi.**	*the-lo na kra-tee-so e-na tra-pe-zee*
The bill, please.	**Ton logariazmó parakaló.**	*ton lo-gar-yas-mo pa-ra-ka-lo*
I am a vegetarian.	**Ímai hortofágos.**	*ee-meh chor-to-fa- gos*
waiter/waitress	**Servitóros/ servitóra**	*ser-vee-tor-oz/ ser-vee-tor-ah*
menu	**O katálogos**	*o ka-ta-lo-gos*
cover charge	**To "couvert"**	*to koo-ver*
wine list	**Lísta krasión**	*lees-ta kra-si-on*
glass	**To potíri**	*to po-tee-ree*
bottle	**To poukáli**	*to bou-ka-lee*
knife	**To mahéri**	*to ma-he-ree*
fork	**To piroúni**	*to pee-roo-nee*
spoon	**To koutáli**	*to koo-ta-lee*
breakfast	**To proïnó**	*to pro-ee-no*
lunch	**To mesi-merianó**	*to me-see-mer-ya-no*
dinner	**To dípno**	*to theep-no*
main course	**To kyríos piáto**	*to kee-ree-os pya-toe*
starters/ first courses	**Ta orektiká**	*ta o-rek-tee-ka*
dessert	**To epidórpia**	*eh-pee-dor-pee-ah*
dish of the day	**To piáto tis iméras**	*to pya-to tees ee-me-ras*
bar	**To "bar"**	*To bar*
taverna	**I tavérna**	*ee ta-ver-na*
café	**To kafenío**	*to ka-fe-nee-o*
fish taverna	**I psarotavérna**	*ee psa-ro-ta-ver-na*
grill house	**I psistariá**	*ee psee-sta-rya*

wine-and-cookhouse	**To inomagerío**	*to ee-no-ma-ye-rio*
dairy shop	**To galakto-poleío**	*to ga-lak-to-po-lee-o*
restaurant	**To estiatório**	*to e-stee-a-to-ree-o*
ouzeri	**To ouzerí**	*to oo-ze-ree*
meze house	**To meze-dopolío**	*To me-ze-do-po-lee-o*
take away souvláki stall	**Ena souvlatzí-diko**	*Eh-na soo-vlat-zee-dee-ko*
take away kebab stall	**Ena kebabtzí-diko**	*Eh-na keh-bahb zee-dee-ko*
take away gyros stall	**Ena gyrádiko**	*Eh-na yeer-ah-dee-ko*
rare	**Eláhista psiméno**	*e-lach-ees-ta psee-me-no*
medium	**Métria psiméno**	*met-ree-a psee-me-no*
well done	**Kalopsiméno**	*ka-lo-psee-me-no*

Basic Food and Drink

coffee	**O Kafés**	*o ka-fes*
with milk	**me gála**	*me ga-la*
coffee without sugar	**skétos horís záhar**	*ske-tos ho-rees za-ha-ree*
medium sweet	**métrios**	*me-tree-os*
very sweet	**glykós**	*glee-kos*
tea	**tsái**	*tsa-ee*
hot chocolate	**zestí sokoláta**	*ze-stee so-ko-la-ta*
wine	**krasí**	*kra-see*
red	**kókkino**	*ko-kee-no*
white	**lefkó**	*lef-ko*
rosé	**rozé**	*ro-ze*
water	**To neró**	*to ne-ro*
octopus	**To chtapódi**	*to chta-po-dee*
fish	**To psári**	*to psa-ree*
cheese	**To tyrí**	*to tee-ree*
halloumi	**To haloúmi**	*to ha-loo-mee*
bread	**To psomí**	*to pso-mee*
fava purée	**I fáva**	*ee fah-va*
halva	**O halvás**	*o hal-vas*
meat slabs	**O gýros**	*o yee-ros*
mince risolles	**Kebab**	*ke-bahb*
Turkish delight	**To loukoúmi**	*to loo-koo-mee*
baklava	**O baklavás**	*o bak-la-vas*

Numbers

1	**éna**	*e-na*
2	**dýo**	*thee-o*
3	**tría**	*tree-a*
4	**téssera**	*te-se-ra*
5	**pénde**	*pen-deh*
6	**éxi**	*ek-si*
7	**eptá**	*ep-ta*
8	**ohtó**	*och-to*
9	**ennéa**	*e-ne-a*
10	**déka**	*the-ka*
11	**énteka**	*en-de-ka*
12	**dódeka**	*tho-the-ka*
13	**dekatría**	*de-ka-tree-a*
14	**dekatéssera**	*the-ka-tes-se-ra*
15	**dekapénde**	*the-ka-pen-de*
16	**dekaéxi**	*the-ka-ek-si*
17	**dekaeptá**	*the-ka-ep-ta*
18	**dekaohtó**	*the-ka-och-to*
19	**dekaennéa**	*the-ka-e-ne-a*
20	**íkosi**	*ee-ko-see*
21	**ikosiéna**	*ee-ko-see-e-na*
30	**triánda**	*tree-an-da*
40	**saránda**	*sa-ran-da*
50	**penínda**	*pe-neen-da*
60	**exínda**	*ek-seen-da*
70	**evdomínda**	*ev-tho-meen-da*
80	**ogdónda**	*og-thon-da*
90	**enenínda**	*e-ne-neen-da*
100	**ekató**	*e-ka-to*
200	**diakósia**	*thya-kos-ya*
1,000	**hília**	*cheel-ya*
2,000	**dýo hiliádes**	*thee-o cheel-ya-thes*
1,000,000	**éna ekatommýrio**	*e-na e-ka-to-mee-ree-o*
one minute	**éna leptó**	*e-na lep-to*
one hour	**mía óra**	*mee-a o-ra*
half an hour	**misí óra**	*mee-see o-ra*
quarter of an hour	**éna tétarto**	*e-na te-tar-to*
half past one	**mía kai misí**	*mee-a keh mee-see*
quarter past one	**mía kai tétarto**	*mee-a keh te-tar-to*
ten past one	**mía kai déka**	*mee-a keh the-ka*
quarter to two	**dýo pará tétarto**	*thee-o pa-ra te-tar-to*
ten to two	**dýo pará déka**	*thee-o pa-ra the-ka*
a day	**mía méra**	*mee-a me-ra*
a week	**mía evdomáda**	*mee-a ev-tho-ma-tha*
a month	**énas mínas**	*e-nas mee-nas*
a year	**énas hrónos**	*e-nas hro-nos*
Monday	**Deftéra**	*thef-te-ra*
Tuesday	**Tríti**	*tree-tee*
Wednesday	**Tetárti**	*te-tar-tee*
Thursday	**Pémpti**	*pemp-tee*
Friday	**Paraskeví**	*pa-ras-ke-vee*
Saturday	**Sávvato**	*sa-va-to*
Sunday	**Kyriakí**	*keer-ee-a-kee*
January	**Ianouários**	*ee-a-noo-a-ree-os*
February	**Fevrouários**	*fev-roo-a-ree-os*
March	**Mártios**	*mar-tee-os*
April	**Aprílios**	*a-pree-lee-os*
May	**Máïos**	*ma-ee-os*
June	**Ioúnios**	*ee-oo-nee-os*
July	**Ioúlios**	*ee-oo-lee-os*
August	**Ávgoustos**	*av-goo-stos*
September	**Septémvrios**	*sep-tem-vree-os*
October	**Októvrios**	*ok-to-vree-os*
November	**Noémvrios**	*no-em-vree-os*
December	**Dekémvrios**	*the-kem-vree-os*